Different Together

Bridges of Mutual Respect

co-authors

Joy Carol and Kyle Reese

with Katie Sanborn-Price

in collaboration with OneJax, Inc.

Praise for *Different Together*

It's exciting to see the OneJax tagline "Different Together" brought to life in this insightful book by Joy Carol and Kyle Reese. The stories contained in these pages are an authentic representation of the type of lives we should – and could – all be living. Here you'll find not only a myriad of voices with inspirational and compassionate tales to tell. You'll also find our aspiration to rise above all else so that we can live with respect and understanding of our neighbors. Different Together *shows us how.*
– Nancy Broner, OneJax Executive Director Emerita

Different Together *has deeply touched my heart. No matter what the culture or faith, these stories have been stimulating and thought provoking. As I read this book, I could see aspects of my own life, faith, and culture. How inspiring and hopeful to see that no matter who we are or what we believe, we can be enriched by stories of others' wisdom, insights, and faiths.*
– Dr. Mobeen Rathore, *Chair of the Board of OneJax, Inc.*

This precious book Different Together *allows you to experience the honesty of deep relationships that cross cultural, religious, and national borders. What a gift to read the varied stories of important relationships that include survival in war-torn areas and immigration to new countries and cultures, as well as evolving respect, dedication and joy in each other's profound differences. Thank you, dear authors, for lifting up these precious souls, so that we may learn more easily what it means to appreciate the gift of differences and the joy of love across all borders and boundaries.*
– Rev. Dr. Victoria R. Sirota, Author, *Preaching to the Choir: Claiming the Role of Sacred Musician*; Episcopal Priest; Musician; Chaplain for The Association of Anglican Musicians.

Different Together opens us up to the beauty that lives in embracing our differences. Through compelling stories, Joy Carol and Kyle Reese show us how we can feel deeper connections with people near and far. In this fascinating exploration, they help us notice the vitally important ways that relationships with people of different backgrounds make life richer and more meaningful. This inspiring book will prompt us all to open up to the world in whole new ways.
– Emily McKhann, Author, *Living with the End in Mind*; Co-founder of "The Motherhood"

What the world needs now more than ever is a lens through which we see our commonalities first. Joy Carol and Kyle Reese have done just that in their beautiful book, Different Together. *Read it, absorb it, and begin to see the world – and each other – in an astoundingly fresh way.*
– Rev. Susan Sparks, Author, *Laugh Your Way to Grace; Reclaiming the Spiritual Power of Humor; Love, a Tiara, and a Cupcake: Three Secrets to Finding Happy*; comedian, preacher.

In this time of collective and global challenge, the vital power of individuals working together has never been more important. This beautiful book captures the grace and power of what can happen when people of different faiths and cultures meet, cherish, and respect each others' differences. Their stories light our way.
– Nina H. Frost, Co-author, *Soul Mapping: An Imaginative Way to Self-Discovery*; Retreat Leader

Joy Carol and Kyle Reese have presented a book that highlights the often-glossed over issues of our time with insightful clarity and wisdom. By showing readers the personal stories of cross-cultural and interreligious friendships and collaborations, Different Together *takes the reader deeper than the common practice of interreligious dialogue that often does not allow enough time for meaningful and sus-*

tainable change. *The stories in* Different Together *let us know that not only can we be different together, but our lives are richer together. These stories are a testament to what is possible across religions and cultures even as we honor our differences.*
– Rev. Dr. Cari Jackson, Author, *Love Like You've Never Been Hurt; The Gift to Listen, the Courage to Hear;* Empowerment Coach, Speaker

This book is a must-read. Unlike much of the current literature concerning interfaith issues, Different Together *offers perspectives based on love and acceptance rather than academic unity. It is personal, moving, and will encourage the reader to seek out and enjoy others of all faiths. The stories of overcoming and melting barriers are not only inspiring, but motivate us to affirmatively accept and cherish each other.*
– Ardith Keef, Author, *The Russian Soldier's Handbook;* Professor Emeritus,
University of Southern Maine

Different Together *is welcome, timely, and inspiring. Stories of friendship and respect between people of very different backgrounds, although unusual and perhaps even surprising, are never out-of-date or out-of-place. When we feel buffeted by events beyond our control, or continue to languish in the sameness of one day following another, Joy Carol and Kyle Reese offer us glimpses of how others have found new stimulation as they made friends with others of different ethnicities or beliefs. What a wonderful way of expanding our own circles of friends and acquaintances!*
– David G. Dickason, author of *Faith, Hope, and Love: The Hakeem's Journey*

In today's too often politicized and fractured world, kudos to Kyle Reese and Joy Carol for Different Together. *This book of stories of friendships among people of diverse religions and cultures highlights how we all can benefit by taking the time*

v

to know people different than ourselves. These poignant stories remind us to remember that we are all part of an interdependent web of existence.
– **Rev. Dr. Debra W. Haffner,** Author, *From Diapers to Dating*; President Emerita, Religious Institute; Unitarian Universalist Minister

Different Together is more than timely. It's essential. Unless we can collectively find a way to consciously seek out and embrace our shared humanity, we may find ourselves at the edge of the precipice. We all live on the same planet and breathe the same air. This powerful book introduces us to positive and forward-looking individuals who show us a way to build bridges. I hope this new, important work will find its way into bookstores everywhere. It just might change the way we see one another.
– **Deirdre Felton**, Retired Thanatologist, Past President of Coastal Family Hospice Board of Directors, Midcoast Maine

Finding opportunities to explore the spiritual journey of other people's faiths and traditions widens one's own world view. Joy Carol and Kyle Reese's new book Different Together gives splendid testimony to those who have done so and nudges others to follow suit. At the same time, the shared stories and the authors' own thoughts remind the reader that personal spiritual growth in one's own faith may also be an unexpected and positive outcome of personally knowing persons who follow different religious paths.
– **Peter J. Purdy**, Past President, The U.S. Committee for the U.N. Population Fund; Past Director, International Programs for Planned Parenthood NY

Different Together is a much-needed book with inspiring stories of people who have found ways to bridge great divides through experiences, friendships, and communities. For anyone concerned about the deep divisions in our own country as well as around the world, this book provides a resource for

bridging divides and enjoying our common humanity.
– **Ellen Kirby,** Editor, *Community Gardening Handbook*;
Writer, Response, United Methodist Women; Past President,
American Community Gardening Association

*Different Together is a book with a crucial message to human-
ity in this time of much division among people. I felt a stirring
in my heart as I read it and thought to myself, "What can I
do to help humanity become a one world family that we long
for?" I am thankful to all who work toward the concept of a
one world family. Joy Carol and Kyle Reese are among those
light-bearers in the steady march towards this ideal. I highly
recommend this uplifting and inspiring book.*
– **Katrina Valenzuela**, Author, *River of Stars, Nights of Jas-
mine.*

*My belief in learning about others is fundamental to my soul.
So I am excited about the work Joy Carol and Kyle Reese
have done creating this book which speaks to our desperate
need for peace in our chaotic world and our true ability to
love and understand one another's lives and belief systems
when given the opportunity to listen and learn. A great book!*
– **Linda M. Ashley**, Retired Director, Social Work Department,
Winthrop University.

*Hooray for this book. We, especially sheltered Americans,
need to embrace diversity and learn from "the other" and
look outward to all of God's children whether they be Muslim, Hindu, Christian, Jewish, Buddhist. We are all part of
God's tribe and should embrace each other and revel in the
diversity. We can learn so much from each other. Thanks for
this exciting book.*
– **Liz Ryder,** Author, *Nursing Times*, "Preying on Your Mind";
School Administrator, Congo

Nothing has been richer for me than the times when Joy Carol shared her experiences as a citizen of the world. I love Different Together, *her latest book coauthored with Kyle Reese. I know everyone will enjoy the many truths they have to share.*
– **Lou Gropp,** Retired Editor-in-Chief, *House & Garden, Elle Decor,* and *House Beautiful.*

Every person everywhere should read this book! People today are afraid and distrustful of those who are different from themselves. These true-life accounts show that knowing people who are different from ourselves makes our lives richer. As we have conversations with others who seem different from us, we open ourselves to the possibility that we may be pleasantly surprised by what we have in common.
– **Martha E. Gale,** Retired Educator of the Blind, Visually Impaired and Learning disabled

When people are being cast as "the other," it is inspiring to be reminded that we are all human beings seeking connection. The rewarding inter-religious and intercultural relationships depicted in this extraordinary book Different Together *exemplify the importance of openness and curiosity, love and forgiveness. Examples of unlikely friendships populate this book and inspire us towards being open and accepting. Read, and be reminded of what is possible in human relations.*
– **Nora Licht,** Educator, Artist, Writer, Immigrant Advocate.

As I read the book Different Together, *coauthored by Joy Carol and Kyle Reese, I found it hard to put down. This book tells the personal stories of how people from different faiths, cultures, and backgrounds come together, first as strangers, then as friends and neighbors. Ultimately, their new common ground encourages the formation of strong bonds and builds community. This book will help us build "bridges of respect"*

when we encounter "differences." Different Together *is enjoyable, valuable, and definitely worth reading.*
– **Dr. Martha (Mickey) Taylor**, Doctorate in Pedagogy and Curriculum Development; Professor Emeritus of Education, Winthrop University.

This well written book on Mutual Respect for others - especially others of differing cultures and faiths - brings home the idea that we are all in this together. That, we are one melting pot of mixed backgrounds, ideas, races, etc. but we are all part of the human race. Through many wonderful and excellent stories, Joy and Kyle have captured the key tenant of faith, regardless of religion. That "God" IS LOVE and while each culture, religion, or faith expresses that in dissimilar ways, we can all identify with that overreaching tenet of LOVE. This book can help open ourselves, through these stories they so wonderfully write, so we can learn and explore how best to accept each other and respect each other. It shows us how we can find the goodness of others even though they appear or do live differently from us. This book helps remind us that we all need each other, and we need to help each other as best we can, for as long as we can, and for as many as we can, even those of different cultures and faiths.
– **David J. Quirk,** Capt. SC, USN Retired

Contents

Contents - cont'd

DEDICATION

This book is dedicated to all who are open to diversity
and are helping to make the world a better place to live.

INTRODUCTION

The basis of world peace is the teaching which runs through almost all the great religions of the world. Love thy neighbor as thyself.

— Eleanor Roosevelt

This book has deeply touched my heart. No matter what the culture or the faith, the stories within this book have been stimulating and thought provoking for me. As I read this book, I could see that the people telling their stories were open to learning from others. And I could also see aspects of my own life, faith, and culture. It made me feel comfortable to join in with persons who seem to be dissimilar from me.

The chapters in this book include stories of people who are Christians, Muslims, Hindus, Jews, Buddhists, and more. As you read their stories, you will see that we can gain so much from one another. Perhaps they will help us to explore our openness to the goodness of others even though they may appear different from us.

This book also put me in mind of the words of Pope Francis who wrote in *Laudato Si'*: "We must regain the conviction that we need one another, that we have a shared responsibility for others and the world, and that being good and decent are worth it." Wise words indeed!

Undoubtedly, we know that we live in a world of many different races, cultures, and faiths. And we are acutely aware that all of us, regardless of our traditions, are confronted with common social and environmental challenges that are complicated and threatening. So, it is important that people of differing cultures and religious traditions learn to respect each other and work together to address these issues. History shows us that positive intercultural and interfaith relationships have been effective in promoting successful human coexistence.

Additionally, there is a deep concern about cultural and religious intolerance in the United States and throughout the world. The abuse of religion has threatened peaceful coexistence everywhere. And political and economic marginalization have generated an atmosphere that permits such problems to flourish. Unfortunately, judging people who are different is far too common and easy to do.

Furthermore, the inappropriate use of religion can lead to self-righteousness and denigration of "the other," thus enabling a group to see itself as more holy or more "chosen." Believing they have a monopoly on the Divine makes it difficult for them to see the work of the Divine in others. This may give rise to a disregard for the religious values of love and forgiveness, which are the core teachings of every major faith.

Rabbi David Rosen, International Director of Interreligious Affairs for the American Jewish Committee, has stated: "Perhaps the greatest challenge for interreligious relationships in our times, is to discover the Divine Presence in each and every person, all created in the Divine image and to receive them accordingly." (*The Challenges of Interfaith Dialogue*)

Certainly, there are differences between various cultures and faiths. However, there are also many similarities. For those who are open to exploring and learning from diversity and new ideas, they might discover that they will develop a deeper appreciation of their own beliefs and culture.

My faith tradition teaches that no person is superior to another based on their race, color of skin, ethnicity, social status, wealth, or country of origin. We are all equal except when based on our actions.

In this book are stories of people who openly reflect on their own faith, as well as their interactions and relationships with people of different traditions than their own. They speak of how they have been inspired, transformed, or challenged by these encounters. They do not necessarily agree on interfaith or inter-cultural connections. But it is inspiring and hopeful to see their positive experiences in each of their stories. Perhaps, no matter who we are or what we believe, we can be enriched by stories of others' wisdom, insights, and faiths.

As you read these narratives, I hope their experiences will be exciting or uplifting for you. May you find a delight in these people who are seeking to discover paths of living in the world in harmony – which perhaps is what we all may be pursuing. Above all, I would like you to enjoy reading each of these special stories.

~ *Dr. Mobeen Rathore,*
Chair of the Board of OneJax, Inc.

JOY CAROL

Open to Change
Co-Author of This Book

*In order to design a future of positive change,
we must first become expert at changing our minds.*
– Jacque Fresco

There are people who are born into isolated communities or locations where there are no other cultures or faiths near them. They might not have exposure to those with unfamiliar or different backgrounds and experiences.

Joy Carol, co-author of this book, was born on a small farm in rural Nebraska, which was located in a place quite isolated from diverse people of other races, cultures, or faiths.

Joy was raised by a supportive, religious Christian family, but they were also receptive to diversity. As she grew up, she had a natural curiosity about life and a desire to be open to other cultures. The call to explore led Joy to work and live in places around the world vastly different from her own.

Through years of positive happenings, events, and exposures in countries around the world, Joy began to see that all people have the potential to care for one another and to live in harmony – to be Different Together.

The experiences and events of her life became opportunities for making changes in her attitudes and understandings. Today she is a woman deeply committed to helping people understand, respect, and honor people of different cultures and faiths.

Joy's Story

My life began on a small farm in rural Nebraska in the middle of the U.S. There in those wide-open spaces, I was reminded that we were just a tiny part of the great cycle of life. My mother and father were generous, wise people, who lovingly cared for the earth and seemed open to new ideas about the world and its peoples. As a result, I grew up with a respect for nature and all people. That Nebraska farmland provided a rich laboratory for my curiosity in life.

My big sister Shirley and I attended a one-room country schoolhouse with ten students in eight grades. We had a tiny "library" with books mostly related to the horse Black Beauty and Dick, Jane, & Spot. When I was about nine, the Farmer's Bank in our local town had a "revolving library" – a box of books that changed every month. In those boxes, I found stories about unusual people and places in the world that I never knew existed. I was mesmerized.

When I was thirteen, my parents sold our farm, and we moved to Lincoln. It was frightening to attend a huge school where we studied weird things like algebra and French. And there were people of color – something I had never seen before.

After high school, I studied education at Wesleyan University and became a teacher in a rather affluent school in Southern California. A colleague teacher constantly bugged me about my bourgeoisie life and challenged me to reach out to people less fortunate than our middle-class students. Because of her tenacity, I volunteered to teach English to Mexican migrant workers – a life-changing experience. My students picked oranges and lived and worked in miserable conditions. But their zest for life was palpable, and their gratitude for learning touched me. It inspired me to apply for a teaching position on a Navajo reservation.

I never made it to the reservation. Another event changed the direction of my life. I met a dynamic woman who had worked in China. She thought my horizons needed to be expanded, that I should be exposed to the "real world" – outside the U.S. She recruited me to work for the Methodist Church in a three-year program similar to the Peace Corps. My assignment: to develop schools and adult literacy programs in some of the poorest communities in the world – the slums of Karachi, West Pakistan, where Muslim refugees from India lived in dilapidated mud huts.

Although I attempted to train for my new assignment, nothing could truly prepare me for my first international work in the slums of Karachi. There I saw poverty, disease, and destitute conditions that I never could have imagined. The neighborhoods where I worked had no electricity, no running water, and no latrines. People had to use the streets as toilets. During the monsoon rains, mud shacks were washed away. Many of the people I worked with were ill, and some had only one meal a day. Young children died from malnutrition and disease.

Yet in the midst of such misery, I experienced a great deal of sharing and joy. Although the children in the mud schoolhouses had no desks or books and sat on gunnysacks on dirt floors, they seemed more enthusiastic about learning than the children I had taught in the affluent school in the U.S.

Often when I visited the neighborhoods where the schools I supervised were located, I was greeted in Urdu, "Memsahib Joy, come have a cup of chai with us." And that literally was one cup. Most of the families in those slums had no cooking facilities nor cups for tea, so someone ran to the bazaar to get one cup of chai.

In sweltering weather, surrounded by open sewers with swarms of flies and mosquitoes, seven or eight of us sat together on the ground and shared that one cup of chai, slowly passing it around and sipping from it. It felt like a gift of camaraderie and hospitality. I was amazed to experience such generosity and delight in those poorest of the poor.

Without a doubt, I enjoyed developing relationships with these extremely poor but astonishingly generous people, who were mostly Muslims. I felt sad when my three years of service ended, and I had to leave my Pakistani friends.

Returning to the U. S., I experienced a bit of culture shock as I tried to adjust to the consumer oriented, fast-paced existence. I'm not sure I ever became entirely accustomed to it.

Soon, I re-embarked on my teaching and counseling career. Although life seemed rich and full, I missed my interactions with people of other cultures and faiths.

I had no idea what was yet to come. Soon doors began to open to interesting international work-related opportunities for organizations such as Save the Children, Christian Children's Fund, the Ford Foundation, the National Council of Churches, and the United Nations. I supervised programs for people in Africa, Asia, and Latin America.

It was exciting and challenging to understand people from many different cultures, customs, and faiths. And it was deeply gratifying and inspiring for me personally. I actually worked for over 35 years around the world. I had been bitten by what I call the "global bug." I felt a sense of camaraderie with the people with whom I worked. They taught me about having an appreciation for life and a *joie de vivre* – no matter what their circumstances, conditions, or faiths.

One of my greatest joys was having the unique opportunity of helping Save the Children to open the first on-the-ground program in Vietnam after the end of the war. It was challenging, complicated, arduous, and fulfilling. I was concerned that I might be seen as "the enemy." I never found that to be the case. The Vietnamese seemed loving and remarkably forgiving for what had been done to their country. People throughout the country wanted to improve the quality of their children's and their own lives, restore their country, and move forward. It was exhilarating to be working where there was great need and where I could make a difference – without trying to change people's style of living or their beliefs.

It was difficult for me to give up this work. I loved being in cultures with people who had different beliefs, religions, values, languages, foods, dreams. I seemed to resonate with them and felt myself developing into an international citizen. I was deeply moved by the people with whom I worked.

It seemed we were all people whose lives could be filled with pain and troubles, but also with joy and love. Without a doubt, I felt we were all children of God.

Finally, after over 35 years of international work, I felt it was important to return to my New York City home and to attend seminary. I wanted to understand how my own spirituality and faith interacted with the many diverse international events I had experienced.

Not long after graduating from seminary, the tragedy of 9/11 shocked the world. Surprisingly, from this disaster emerged a feeling of compassion and cooperation throughout New York City. Volunteers appeared from every culture, ethnic group, faith, class, and profession. Everyone wanted to help in some way.

A new spirit seemed to take over the city. Strangers of all beliefs and cultures embraced one another and cried together. A new respect for different peoples emerged. Churches, synagogues, mosques, and temples learned what it meant to be of service. The oldest church in Manhattan – St. Paul's Chapel, which stood next to the Twin Towers – was one of the examples. After the disaster, it was turned into a house of hospitality for all people. As a Red Cross Chaplain, I saw hundreds of people from all backgrounds enter that space for food, encouragement, and love. The experience of working with people of all cultures and faiths during a challlenging time was inspirational and meaningful.

Yes, looking back, I believe all of these experiences have helped me to cultivate an open, embracing heart. I now feel an empathy for all people no matter what their culture or faith. In addition, I have gained an abundance of joy and a deepening of my own faith. I am very grateful to have had these opportunities, which have enriched my life.

KYLE REESE

New Perceptions and Understandings

Co-Author of This Book, Director of OneJax

It is entirely possible that behind the perception of our senses, worlds are hidden away, and we are unaware.
– Albert Einstein.

There are times in our life when we can be completely surprised. New exposures, new ideas, new experiences can change how we feel about the world and about people who seem different.

Unfortunately, changing our minds can often be difficult for us. It's not easy to open our hearts and our opinions to new perspectives. We tend to like to hang onto what we know or what we are familiar with. However, if we are exposed to ideas and thoughts that are different or unusual to us, we may discover that we might gain new positive perceptions and understandings.

In this chapter, we hear the story of Kyle Reese, who is currently the Director of OneJax, a nonprofit organization in Jacksonville, Florida, that seeks to promote diversity as a foundation for a strong community. What is interesting about this story is that Kyle grew up in a rural Texas community, and his Christian parents were quite conservative in their beliefs.

Through exposure and learning of new, creative, and inspirational ideas from professors, friends, and colleagues, Kyle's perspective on the world changed. As he became friends with people of various denominations, faiths, and cultures, he had an interest in learning from "the others."

As the Director of OneJax, Kyle's story is interesting. OneJax works to increase respect and improve relationships among people who represent the rich menagerie of religious, racial, and cultural groups that compose the community around Jacksonville. The organization is dedicated to achieving understanding, civility, and respect for all peoples, and to being an inclusive community where differences are welcomed and celebrated.

Enjoy the story of Kyle's journey from rural Texas to being the pastor of one of the largest churches in Jacksonville to becoming the Director of OneJax.

Kyle's Story

Today I am the Director of OneJax, a nonprofit organization that seeks to promote diversity as the foundation for a strong community.

At times, I wonder how this could have happened – that I am the director of such an organization. After all, I was born in a tiny rural community outside of Amarillo, Texas. My parents were members of a small Southern Baptist Church, which was quite conservative in its theology and practices.

As I was growing up, I was very active in the life of this church. I helped lead youth groups, taught Sunday school classes, and led Bible studies. I fully participated in every aspect of that church. Often, looking back, I think that all of the activity and involvement there helped lead me to become a minister.

After I graduated from high school, I became a student at Wayland Baptist University, where I studied Christian education and theology. I found many of the professors there quite open minded. They seemed to respect and give life to many things including journalism, music, and education.

During my years at Wayland, many changes were occurring in the Southern Baptist Church. There appeared to be a concerted effort by the fundamentalist leaders of the church to get members on the boards of all the local churches. They were white men, and they were like-minded.

It was at that point that I got involved with founding an organization to stand up against this takeover within the Southern Baptist church. Our group was called "Baptists Committed," and we were very active in Texas and Virginia. We worked with churches and pastors trying to mentor them to be faithful to the Gospel and to push back against fundamentalism.

Several of my professors at Wayland, particularly Professor Gary Manning and Professor Paul Sadler, were very open-minded and gracious. They played a big role in broadening my worldview.

After graduating from Wayland with a bachelor degree in religious education, I went to work part time as a youth minister.

I was planning to go to Southwestern Seminary to study. However, with the assistance of Milton Cunningham, who served as Chaplain and Sports Chaplain at Baylor University and as President of the Baptist General Convention of Texas, I had the opportunity to be in the inaugural class of George W. Truett Seminary at Baylor University in Waco, Texas. At Truett Seminary, theological education is viewed as a sacred process of preparation and transformation. Truett students are taught to think theologically, practice ministry skills, grow spiritually, and to cultivate community.

It was exciting to be in that large university and to experience new remarkable ideas at the Truett Seminary. I had extraordinary classmates from various backgrounds, and we were exposed to amazing people such as Barbara Brown Taylor. It was like experiencing the whole world – and not just a small corner of it. My perspectives on life and on faith were broken open.

When I graduated from Truett Seminary, I realized how much I had been exposed to, how much I had learned, how much my perspectives on life had changed. It had made me be a more open person to the world and especially to other people who were different from me.

Upon graduation I spent five years as a pastor at Valley Mills Texas Baptist Church. It was a very global minded church, and it was another growing experience for me. I'm grateful for those people who stretched my mind.

When I was 31, I was invited to San Angelo Texas First Baptist Church. I remember being a bit nervous, as I was to preach in front of 922 people who would listen to me and then decide if I was to be their senior pastor. After passing their approval, I spent the next 5 1/2 years there with some tough days. There were also many good days while serving as the senior pastor.

All of these varied experiences were increasing my openness and changing my mind about life and some of my earlier rather limited beliefs. Also, I found I was developing an acceptance of other people who had different ideas about their religion or faith than I did.

Then I was called to the Hendricks Avenue Baptist Church in Jacksonville, Florida in 2006 and stayed there for 14 years. That church was a part of the "Cooperative Baptists."

At Hendricks Avenue Baptist there were so many opportunities that I could pursue. I found myself working with other clergy to get us involved in the activities of our churches and our congregations. Perhaps more importantly, we worked together to be deeply involved in the relationship of our churches with the community and with the city of Jacksonville.

One of the really exciting things that happened for me was when the neighboring Jewish temple Ahavath Chesde and Hendricks Avenue Baptist Church began to form a relationship. Ahavath Chesde Temple in Jacksonville is the center of Reform Judaism in Northeast Florida and is committed to the principles of inclusion, compassion, and kindness – starting in the Jacksonville community. The Temple extends a special invitation to interfaith families.

Soon I became very close friends with the rabbis at the Temple, and we did pulpit exchanges. A rabbi would come to preach at Hendricks Avenue Church on a Sunday, and I would preach at the Temple on a Friday night. It was a very exciting time.

Shortly after that, I became good friends with the Imam from the Jacksonville Islamic Center, whose mission statement is to provide holistic religious, social, and educational services fostering devotion towards the worship of God and to be faithful and productive members of American society. We became very good friends and have remained that to this day.

In 2009, I was asked to join the Board of OneJax. It was such an exciting time because interfaith relationships were beginning to flourish and there was a lot of interfaith dialogue going on along with multifaith worship experiences.

OneJax was an amazing organization, expressing its deep appreciation of all people and the sacredness of every person. I felt a true connection to its mission.

Finally, one day, I realized that it was time to have new leadership within the church where I worked. And I felt strongly that I was supposed to help make the city of Jacksonville a better place. So, when I was asked to take the position of the Director of OneJax, I accepted.

I now understand and strongly believe that there is much to gain by living in a multifaith world. It's important for all of us to be open to one another and to appreciate our unique gifts and contributions that each of us makes to the world.

Finally, I also know that by appreciating and accepting other peoples' customs, faiths, and beliefs, it has truly strengthened my own.

LOWEY & SHADIA

Soul Sisters

Third Culture Kid, World as Family

A Third Culture Kid builds relationships to all of the cultures, while not having full ownership in any. The sense of belonging is in relationship to others of similar backgrounds.
– David C. Pollock

Every now and then we hear about "third culture kids" (TCKs) – children who have been born or moved in and out of countries as their parents transferred around the world. Third culture kids are usually the children of diplomats, international business people, missionaries, the military, and people who have relocated because of job placements.

When a child is born and raised in one culture, its identity may be closely aligned with the people from that culture. For many third culture kids, there are benefits. They have the opportunity to learn of other cultures, languages, faiths. They can feel like citizens of the world.

However, some third culture kids feel out of place, struggle with culture shock, and might not have a sense of belonging or being connected. They may suffer from a sense of detachment. Transitions can cause grief-related losses of friends, community, pets, language, food, culture, and a lack of identity.

Lowey Dickason is a third culture kid born in Kuwait and raised in Oman and India by her parents who were both TCKs themselves. They spent their formative years absorbing the same cultures where she lived.

Lowey adapted well to her life and had a greater sense of being "at home" in those environments than many other TCKs. Perhaps it was because her parents were already acquainted with foreign languages and other cultural norms and had family still living in the Gulf and India.

From her cross-cultural and interfaith experiences, Lowey made a "soul sister" (which she describes as a heartfelt relationship based on shared values of what is true and lasting) with Shadia Kanaan, an American Muslim Palestinian.

Lowey's Story

I am a descendent of generations of medical missionaries, who lovingly served the natives of the Persian/Arabian Gulf and India – a TCK daughter of two TCK parents seeped in other cultures.

My parents, Dr. William Wells Thoms and his wife Beth learned Arabic and became familiar with Arab and Indian culture. My dad first practiced in Bahrain and Kuwait (where I was born in 1938). My parents then spent the rest of their careers in Oman, a country my dad knew as a child.

Throughout the 1940's and into the mid 50's, my dad was essentially the only doctor in the entire country where travel was mostly by camel and donkey, and there were no telephones or air conditioning. I accompanied my parents in 1953 on a trip into interior Oman, where Dad operated on an imam's eyes. We spent days traveling by camel and donkey. Mom and I wore native clothes, since the natives had not seen Western women before.

Mom worked full time, keeping accounts for the hospital and overseeing the storeroom for medications and supplies. She also visited folks in the hospital and in their homes, reading scripture and singing hymns, which they seemed to enjoy. She taught Arabic writing and reading to men and women patients being treated for leprosy in the contagious diseases hospital that my dad had built in the late 40's.

When I lived in Oman, my association with native friends was before school age. My sandbox playmates were the children of the hospital workers. I learned a simple child's Arabic, since their parents were Baluchi and Persian, so they spoke Persian at home. Arabic was their second language. No one spoke a word of English. Since there was no school for my siblings and me to attend, we were sent to boarding school in Kodai, South India.

I had a loving former slave woman named Haseena for my ayah. I loved her dearly. Her native language was Swahili, but she spoke a primitive Arabic and a few words of English to me.

As a descendent of generations of medical missionaries, I have experienced God's unconditional embrace of all people. I believe that my interfaith perspectives come more from simply growing up in diversity and squaring that with my convictions about a loving God.

I have friends of other faiths that I embrace as my "soul sisters and brothers." I believe Jesus would embrace them too. Jesus' message concerned God's unconditional, ever-present and everlasting love. Rather than being exclusive, it was inclusive. I believe Jesus would claim as His own all who live by the Commandments of love for God and neighbor, no matter what their faith.

The common basis of faith in one God that the Abrahamic faiths of Judaism, Christianity, and Islam share is found in Genesis 1:26: "Then God said, 'Let us make mankind in our image, in our likeness...' "

The following story bears out the commonality in the Abrahamic faiths. Community (formerly Christian) Peacemaker

Teams (CPT) were formed by the Mennonites, Church of the Brethren, and the American Friends Service Committee. CPT sends teams trained in nonviolent intervention and ministries of presence into explosive situations, to attempt to transform violence into peace.

CPT members were sent to Iraq. On March 29, 2003, deported by Iraqi authorities, CPT members began the 500-mile drive from Baghdad to Amman, Jordan. The taxi, with multinational CPT members, was 75 miles from Jordan when a tire exploded, flipping it into a deep ditch. Two people were seriously injured.

Three Iraqi men, headed to Baghdad, stopped and assisted them into their truck. The CPT members were driven to a station wagon, where they were taken to the wrecked hospital in Rutba, bombed three days earlier. Devoid of anesthesia and equipment, Dr. Farouq Al Dulaimi and the remaining hospital staff bandaged their wounds. The townpeople brought blankets and cared for them until they were strong enough to go to Jordan.

Based on this same respect, Women in Black was started by Israeli Jewish and Palestinian women in 1989 to end the Israeli occupation, stating, "We refuse to be enemies." I've stood with Women in Black in Kalamazoo and also in the middle of Jerusalem.

One of my soul sisters is Shadia Kanaan, an American Palestinian Muslim. I met Shadia when she spoke about Islam at our church in the late 90's. We hit it off right away and became close when we were active with the Kalamazoo Nonviolent Opponents of War after 2003 – through the Women in Black group that she started and I joined.

Shadia has dedicated her life to pursuing peace and justice. She protested the war in Iraq by standing as a Woman in Black holding a sign, "We Mourn All Victims of War and Occupation."

Shadia and I have prayed the Lord's Prayer in Arabic together. She learned the Lord's Prayer when attending a Quaker school in Ramalla. She has no difficulty praying those words of Jesus. And I am comfortable saying the Muslim grace before meals. We often pray for each other. Shadia blessed me when I prepared to go on a CPT delegation to Israel/Palestine. I gave Shadia my mom's Arabic Bible.

Like her fellow Muslims, Shadia takes her obligations toward the poor very seriously through service and financial contributions. She practices hospitality, sharing her home with many.

Islamic society has been falsely labeled "terrorist" before and after 9/11. The word Islam means "one who is submissive to God," which is in keeping with Jesus' teachings about caring for "the least of these my brethren," which was also preached by Mohammad. The Quran actually condemns violence: "Whoever slays a soul, it is as though he slew all men; and whoever keeps one alive, it is as though he kept all alive." There is an obligation in Islam to greet the stranger, even an enemy, as a worthy human who also was made in God's image, and so requires hospitality.

Perhaps the best way to help people understand how those who differ in their faiths and traditions can be good friends is by listening to the words of my soul sister, Shadia Kanaan.

As I ponder her meaningful words, I know why we are soul sisters. I am grateful to have the privilege of being her friend with whom I can share my faith, and she can share hers. By doing so we learn about God's love for all people, since we are all precious creations of God.

Here is what Shadia has said about her faith, affirming all people as made in God's image.

Shadia's Story

I am a Muslim Palestinian American. I want to share what is important to me as a Muslim living in the United States. I have lived in Kalamazoo, Michigan, with my husband, neurologist Dr. Azzaam Kanaan, who was the executive director of KNI/Southwest Michigan Imaging Center. His leadership and commitment to excellence helped keep patient care in the forefront throughout the many medical advances over the years.

My husband and I were born in our native city of Nablus, Palestine, which is famous for its olive oil soap production and a plant that is owned by my family. It was located near my husband's 600-year-old ancestral home, which was bombed, destroying the soap factory and the house with it. My husband and I have lived in Kalamazoo nearly 40 years, built a family and a life, and felt very much at home as a part of this community. It gave us much, and in return we have given back a lot to it.

Until recently, religious differences were a point of interest to most, an intellectual discourse, an enriching dialogue. However, in the recent political climate, Muslims in the United States have lost the comfort of inclusiveness and have begun to feel like the suspected outsider.

I want to emphasize the distinction between Islam, the religion, and the behavior of some Muslims. Extremist acts of violence in the name of religion are not exclusive to Muslims. As history has showed us, religion was the excuse for many wars of expansion and colonialism. Islam became a target even before the attacks on 9/11.

I believe the real problem is fundamentalism, whether it is Jewish, Christian, Hindu, Muslim, or any other. The problem with fundamentalism is that its proponents use their holy messages in a selective manner to suit their agenda. They perceive themselves as part of a cosmic struggle between good and evil in which they find an opponent to demonize in order to defeat that opponent. Examples of the use of religious scriptures to justify wars of conquest and expansion have been evident throughout history. From the Spanish Inquisition to 9/11, the road is full of innocent blood.

As history has witnessed, what unites us as Christians and Muslims is the driving force behind all social movements throughout human history – the need for social change. Awareness and movements at the grassroots level were the impetus for revolutionary change in pursuit of social justice, more equitable distribution of wealth, and respect for human dignity.

I believe there is a deep connection and parallel between the rise of Christianity and Islam as two social movements that have changed the course of human history. I have a deep reverence for the sacred or divine nature of both Jesus and Mohammad. Both of these leaders changed the world. They hoped for a more just social order and were revolutionary in spirit and action.

Mohammad grew up as part of the privileged tribe of Quraish. But out of his sense of human justice, he opposed the materialistic pleasure-seeking values of his time, the disparity of wealth, the unjust distribution of tribal wealth, the constant state of war between the tribes, the valued culture of vengeance, and social ills – from loan sharks, infanticide, drunkenness and gambling, the ill treatment of women, the rampant slavery, and more. Jesus came for the salvation of all people, not limited to one region or one sector or one tribe. He preached his message to a loyal group.

Both prophets threatened the status quo of entrenched interests of the elite and the clergy. Both were fought, persecuted, and threatened. Jesus was crucified. Mohammad's life was threatened with assassination attempts. A state of siege was imposed on him and his followers. He and a few of his loyal followers migrated to Medina in the year 622 CE. When he returned to Mecca 10 years later and was secure in his prevailing message, he waged peace, not war, and his message became public and spread all over Arabia.

Jesus' message found its roots, mainly after his resurrection, through his disciples and ultimately hundreds of years later when the Roman Emperor Constantine made it the official religion of the Roman Empire. It remains a universal standard for spiritual ethics practiced as the largest religion in the world.

Mohammad's message succeeded in his lifetime, which made him a statesman in charge of Umma, a nation. Secular laws had to be legislated to run an organized and controlled state of affairs, which became what we know as Islamic Law. Besides the spiritual message that was revealed upon him by God through the holy book, the Quran, Mohammad was at the realm of historical social revolutionary leadership. In his farewell speech in 632 CE, Mohammad stated: "To be good, not to violate each other's rights, to be good to one's brothers and sisters and put an end to revenge, blood, and vendettas."

So, works of justice were of utmost importance. Other values took a second place – such as wealth, country, family, war, love, and patriotism. In the Quran there is a universal message that transcends gender, nation, tribe, language, color, or even particular religious denominations. It reads: "Righteousness is not turning your faces in the direct of the East or the West. But the righteous are whoever acknowledges God; and spends wealth out of love for relatives, orphans, the poor, the wayfarer, those who ask, and for those in bondage. They establish prayer and pay alms; honoring the covenants they have made persevering in adversity and bad times. These are the trustworthy and these are the ones who have faith."

CHERIAN THOMAS & IAN ZACHARIAH

Lifelong Friends

A Christian and A Jew

It is only the great hearted who can be true friends.
The mean and cowardly, can never know what true friendship means.
– Charles Kingsley

Friendship is often characterized by openness and flexibility. A friend is a person with whom we have a deep, intentional, and intimate relationship.

There are wise people who have suggested that every person should seek at least one friend from another religion or faith. A friendship with someone of another faith can open one's heart. They've added that it only takes one interfaith friend to deepen one's understanding, change one's attitudes of prejudice and discrimination, and broaden one's horizons.

People who have developed interfaith, relationships or friendships understand that, although their beliefs may be different, they most likely share common purposes and goals – such as living in harmony, being good citizens, leading an ethical life.

At times, friendships that are experienced between people of different faiths can last a lifetime. Such relationships are usually based on a sense of trust, common interests, and a respect for the other person's faith without any thought or effort

28

to convert or change the other person's beliefs.

In this story of Ian Zachariah, a Jew living in Kolkata (Calcutta), India, and Cherian Thomas, an Indian Christian now living in the U.S., their friendship started in 1951 when they were young children attending school together in Jamshedpur, India. Their relationship has continued over the decades right up to present times. They keep their friendship alive through regular WhatsApp phone conversations and occasional reunions with their classmates, who are also people of different faiths.

Their friendship has been a source of great benefit and joy for both Ian and Cherian.

Cherian's Story

I was born in Jamshedpur near Kolkata in 1943. My parents were from Kerala and were Christians, descendants of those converted by St. Thomas in AD 52. They moved to Jamshedpur, Bihar State in Eastern India in 1939, soon after their marriage. My father, who had a degree in chemistry, got a job in the steel melting unit in the Tata Iron & Steel Company (TISCO).

Jamsetji Tata had founded the company in 1907 when India was under British rule. Mr. Tata was a Parsi (an ethnoreligious group on the Indian subcontinent which descended from Persians, who had migrated to Medieval India in order to preserve their Zoroastrian identity). He was a socially conscious man. He spelt out his concept of a township for the workers at the company in a letter he wrote to his son in 1902, five years before even a site for the company had been decided.

"Be sure to lay wide streets planted with shady trees, every other of a quick-growing variety. Be sure there is plenty of space for lawns and gardens. Reserve large areas for football, hockey and parks. Earmark areas for Hindu temples, Mohammedan mosques and Christian churches".

TISCO invited the American Jesuits from Calcutta to start a school and they did so in 1947. I joined the Loyola High School in 1951 in grade one and went right through high school. We were taught by American Jesuits and Indian teachers in a curriculum from Cambridge University.

Boys of all faiths attended the school including Parsis, Hindus, Muslims, Sikhs, Jews, and Christians. We got along very well together and participated in various kinds of sports. We treated each other with respect. It didn't matter that we had different faiths. We felt we were all together.

One of my classmates who became my good friend and continues to be my friend was Ian Zachariah, an Indian Jew, who went on to work in advertising in Kolkata. I was pleased to see a New York Times story in 2008 about his efforts to look after the three synagogues in Kolkata.

Ian and I would like to share the story of our lives and our friendship over the years.

Ian's Story

In the 18th century, my ancestors came to India from Aleppo, which was a Syrian city. Others came from Iran and Iraq. They were known as Baghdadi Jews in India.

I have lived in Kolkata all my life. I have a son in Germany, a daughter in the U.K., and a brother in London.

When my family first came to India, it was one of the few places in the world that was hospitable to Jews. So, they came to British India as exporters, real-estate dealers, and bakers, trading in spices, tobacco, tea, textiles, and jewels. They made a name as exporters and real-estate dealers and bakers. Usually, they lived in neighborhoods in the central city. They built lovely buildings in Badabazaar, Kolkata's largest wholesale market.

Eventually the Jewish settlers in Kolkata built synagogues, a hospital, and schools. Although there is not one student who is Jewish attending the schools, they still are in operation.

Nahoum and Sons established a landmark bakery in New Market. It too, like every other Jewish institution, faces a risky future. One of the last family members who owned the bakery died in 2013. His brother comes to visit the employees from time to time who still operate the bakery.

In 1947, there were around 12,000 Baghdadi Jews in all of India. Those numbers have now dwindled down to only a few hundred. In a nation of more than a billion people, the Jews don't even qualify as a minority group anymore. In Kolkata, the Jewish community at one time was thriving with about 5,000 to 6,000 members. During World War II, the population grew when Jews from Burma and Europe moved to the city seeking refuge. Today I think there are less than 30 Jews left in the city.

For many years, I have been involved with the beautiful Maghen David Synagogue. I was a child when my grand-uncle first took me to services there. Maghen David is one of the synagogues which still exists today but more as a memorial to an earlier time than as a functional Jewish temple. In that synagogue, there have not been many prayers said in a long time. We rarely have 10 able-bodied men needed to form the minyan, the quorum required for a Jewish service. Magen David and the city's two other synagogues used to be packed on Jewish holidays.

Today the caretakers of the Maghen David Synagogue are third generation Muslims who have lovingly cared for the place for years. One of the guards, who took over the job from his father, stated his commitment to preserve the memory of Kolkata's Jews. "I know the Jewish holidays, and my father taught me all the Jewish namaz (the Urdu word for prayers). Whether Jews come or not, we will still be here to watch over this place for them."

Kolkata was the kind of place that absorbed everyone and

was tolerant of differences. On the same corner as Maghen David Synagogue, land was shared by a Christian church, a Hindu shrine, and a Muslim mosque.

Many Jews began leaving the city after Indian independence in 1947. Also, Israel became an independent country in 1948. So many people left the country to emigrate to Israel, the U.K., Australia, Canada, and the U.S. Unfortunately, those who remained are slowly dying off.

Looking back to the time when Cherian and I were class-mates in the school in Jamshedpur, it was a wonderful time. Although my family was the only Jewish family in the city, and my two brothers and I were the only Jewish students in the Loyola School, there were no problems. We weren't bothered by one another. We cared for one another and celebrated festivals together.

Today in the world, there seem to be more thoughts and questions about where people are from, what is their religion, how are they behaving?

I am grateful for my wonderful friendship with Cherian and others in our class who were of different faiths. I believe we will always care for one another.

GEORGE HULL

Navigating Sectarian Waters

From the Shadows of Belfast's Shipyards to a Transformative Faith

If you want to make peace with your enemy, you have to work with your enemy. Then he becomes your partner.
- Nelson Mandela

Every person is born as a blank slate, a canvas waiting to be painted with the brushstrokes of life's experiences. In those earliest moments, we exist in a state of unity with our mothers. The awakening to our identity occurs over time.

As we emerge from infancy, we become aware of the societal tapestry into which we are woven. Our family of origin becomes the loom upon which our earliest perceptions, values, and beliefs are woven. We inherit a worldview that is linked to the social, cultural, and national contexts that frame our lives. Family traditions, stories, and experiences shape the lens through which we view the world.

Just as our genetic inheritance influences the color of our eyes, our political inclinations are often inherited. Our family's political milieu shapes our early understanding of governance, societal roles, and power dynamics. Similarly, the religious narratives are often rooted in our families' traditions.

However, as we journey through life, we may encounter crossroads that invite us to question the inherited narratives and worldviews that have shaped us. Self-discovery becomes a process of deconstruction sifting through the layers of inherited beliefs to discern what resonates with our true selves. This journey is often characterized by introspection, unlearning, and a willingness to embrace new perspectives.

On this journey, we realize we have the power to engage in critical reflection, question assumptions, and explore alternative narratives. As we cast off preconceived notions and dare to venture into the uncharted territories of individual thought, we can grow and transform.

In the end, the journey from inherited identity to authentic selfhood is a profound exploration. It is a dance between the canvas provided by our family and our culture and the brushstrokes we add through our experiences.

In this amazing story, George Hull, who lived in Northern Ireland during the difficult days of the Troubles, talks about the unique path that he has taken to uncover the truths that define him as a man who has become ecumenical and interfaith.

George's Story

In the heart of East Belfast, beneath the imposing presence of Harland & Wolff's shipyard cranes, the intricate threads of my childhood were woven against a tapestry dominated by sectarianism and religious fundamentalism.

This was the very place where the majestic Titanic was brought to life, but its colossal shadow was eclipsed by the intricate political divisions that had perennially estranged the Protestant and Roman Catholic communities of Northern Ireland.

Growing up amidst the clangor of Belfast's industrial landscape, I was acutely aware that my religious identity extended beyond a personal belief – it wielded political clout. The subtle interplay between religious fundamentalism and political authority shaped the landscape, with carefully manipulated borders ensuring Protestant ascendancy. From my earliest years, I internalized the notion that Roman Catholics weren't just distinct in their beliefs; they were adversaries, both religious and political.

Raised within the modest confines of a working-class household, my exposure to formal education was limited. University education felt like an elusive dream, reserved for others more privileged. Books were scarce, overshadowed by the prestige of manual trades. My parents, nominal Protestants, adhered to rituals like baptism, driven more by tradition than spiritual conviction.

In the midst of fervent religious symbols, with open Bibles and parades flaunting Protestant pride and domination, simmering tensions lay concealed – readily poised to erupt into the sectarian violence that would define the era.

A mother burdened by chronic asthma and a father finding solace in weekend drinking; our household knew anxiety well. Silence and secrecy became our armor, as we weathered the storms of a society steeped in violence and the inner struggles of a working-class family who had more in common with their Roman Catholic neighbors than their Protestant culture would allow.

As a young lad, I navigated the labyrinthine streets, retrieving my father from pubs on Friday nights, carrying back the earnings that barely sustained us through the week and in a household where cigarettes were considered an essential.

Simultaneously, Sunday school and religious rites acted as poignant reminders of a faith polarized and divisive. Lessons of sin and redemption from well-intentioned Sunday school teachers tangled my understanding of self and spirituality further.

The 1960s in Northern Ireland were characterized by turmoil, with echoes of past battles reverberating through the streets in chants of "No Surrender" and "We are the People."

Amid bombings, shootings, and loss, I left school at age fifteen to join the workforce as a bricklayer. It was while serving my time as an apprentice bricklayer that I met Paddy Connolly, a journeyman who taught me the skill of laying bricks.

Paddy was a Roman Catholic and there is no doubt that he cared for me and only wanted the best for me as he translated the skill of his craftsmanship to my own clumsy hands.

He challenged my embedded concept that Roman Catholics were my enemies, Paddy was like a second father to me and to be sure I knew his love and regard to *be sure.*

For me, amidst all the chaos that was Northern Ireland, the clubs and pubs of East Belfast offered a momentary reprieve from the despair of the violence that was everyday life.

Turning back to the faith of my childhood in search of solace and purpose, a chance encounter with Brian Ervine, a well know Christian presence in the community, set me on a different course. Committing my life to Christ on an ordinary street corner marked a transformative pivot. Brian's guidance gently nudged me away from the limitations of sectarianism, toward a broader understanding of a more inclusive faith.

Engaging in countless conversations and shared reflections, Brian challenged the biases etched into my psyche since childhood. He introduced me to literature, philosophy, and theology, igniting an insatiable curiosity about the world. The rigid walls of religious dogma began to crumble, revealing a panorama of compassion, empathy, and unity that had eluded me.

Emboldened by Brian's encouragement, I embarked on an educational journey, turning away from evenings in pubs to immerse myself in books. The university, once an unattainable mirage, now beckoned with boundless opportunities. The hands that once laid bricks now flipped through pages brimming with thoughts and ideas that expanded my horizons.

As I delved deeper into learning, I realized that the chasms dug by religious and political ideologies weren't unassailable truths. They were constructs susceptible to deconstruction through dialogue and understanding. The sectarian strife entangling Northern Ireland was not a manifestation of intrinsic differences, but a heartbreaking outcome of fear, misinformation, and historical grievances.

With each newfound insight, my heart expanded. Reaching across the aisle, I reached out to both Catholic and Protestant communities, seeking commonalities over contrasts. Engaging in interfaith discussions, I discovered that the boundary between "us" and "them" was blurrier than I'd been led to believe. The interactions weren't void of challenges, yet they were profoundly transformative.

In the early 1970s, amidst escalating Troubles, a new calling emerged: peace activism. The very streets that had been synonymous with divisions now stood as stages for unity and reconciliation. Shoulder to shoulder with a diverse cohort, I sought peace and mutual understanding, striving to put an end to the bloodshed that had plagued our society.

The transformation from a youth entangled in divisive sectarian currents to a peace advocate yearning for shared humanity was riddled with obstacles. It necessitated shedding deep-seated prejudices, confronting personal biases, and embracing the vulnerability of transformation. Amid it all, redemption's power emerged – not in a theological sense, but in humanity's capacity to change, evolve, and heal.

As I stood on that transformative street corner, committing my life to Christ, I could never have anticipated the odyssey awaiting me. From the shadow of Belfast's great shipyard cranes to the pursuit of knowledge and the quest for peace, my narrative wove into Northern Ireland's evolving story. Though the door to my past firmly shut, what lay beyond was a realm of growth, understanding, and an unwavering belief that transformation can flourish, even in the direst circumstances.

From my upbringing during Northern Ireland's late 1960s to the tumultuous 1990s, I've intimately experienced the pitfalls of religious and cultural polarization. Guided by my Methodist faith and commitment to Christ, I stand unwaveringly dedicated to ecumenism.

Engaging in profound dialogues with neighbors of differing faiths, I have learned that we can harness our unique mission's essence to foster mutual understanding, cooperation, and transformation. By learning from our neighbors of diverse faiths, I believe we enrich our own spiritual journey and fortify our testament to a world yearning for unity, compassion, and love.

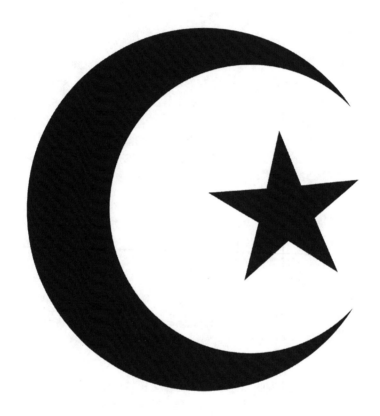

DR. MOBEEN HASAN RATHORE

Getting Involved with Those Different from You

Chair of the Board of OneJax, Inc.

*When you do nothing, you feel overwhelmed and powerless.
But when you get involved, you feel the sense of hope
that comes from knowing you are working to make things better.*
– Anonymous

Dr. Mobeen Hasan Rathore is an amazing, brilliant man. He not only is professor and associate chair at the Department of Pediatrics at the University of Florida. He also is the chief of the Division of Pediatric Infectious Diseases and Immunology as well as Director of the University of Florida Center for HIV/ AIDS research, education, and service (UF CARES). And he is a pediatrician at the Wolfson Children's Hospital in Jacksonville, Florida. His clinical special interests include immunizations, pediatric HIV and infectious diseases in children. He speaks English, Urdu, and Punjabi.

Dr. Rathore was born in Lahore, Pakistan and is a Muslim. He is a man of deep courage and insight. He not only yearns for but works for a world that is inclusive and beyond boundaries of religions, customs, and cultures.

Perhaps one of the best descriptions of Dr. Rathore is that he gets involved and actively participates in many important aspects of community life and living. He is open with his opinions and courageous enough to speak his wise and inspirational thoughts without fear.

Dr. Rathore is the President of OneJax, a nonprofit Institute that seeks to promote diversity as the foundation for a strong community by working to increase respect and improve relationships among people who represent the rich menagerie of religious, ethnic, racial, and cultural groups that compose the community of Jacksonville, Florida.

His story shows us a potent concept of insight and strength. Most importantly, it encourages us to be open and involved with those who are different from ourselves.

Dr. Rathore's Story

I was born in 1959 in the beautiful city of Lahore, Pakistan. I came to the United States over 40 years ago and have been living here ever since. For the last 32 years, I have been working in Jacksonville Florida as a pediatrician. I presently am on the faculty of the University of Florida College of Medicine, Jacksonville, teaching pediatrics. I also work as a medical doctor at Wolfson Children's Hospital in Jacksonville.

I feel very fortunate that my life has been extremely interesting and mostly quite pleasant. Oh yes, there have been times when there were problems or difficulties for me or my family or for people of my Islamic faith. But on the whole, it's been a very positive, inspirational, and hope-filled life.

In my early years in Pakistan, I received my education at an excellent boarding school Lawrence College in Ghora Gali, in the Himalayan mountains in northern Pakistan. This school was founded in 1860. At the school, most of the children were Muslims from Pakistan. But there also were a few other international children of other faiths. However, there never seemed to be any serious problems.

After graduation, I studied at the King Edward Medical University (KEMU), which is a public medical university located in Lahore, Pakistan. KEMU was founded in 1860 by the British Raj and was named after King Edward VII. After Pakistan's independence in 1947, the university became the only medical college in the province. At KEMU, I chose to study pediatrics focusing on infectious diseases for children.

When I graduated from medical school, I was given the opportunity to do research in the United States at the Cincinnati Children's Hospital and Medical Center. The focus of my research was on pediatric infectious diseases – especially on whooping cough, which is so prevalent among children of Pakistan and other parts of the world. That was a very interesting time for me.

Then I went on to the Akron Children's Hospital and Medical Center in Ohio as a resident. After Akron, I was given a fellowship to work with pediatric infectious diseases at the St. Louis University School of Medicine and at Washington University in St. Louis, Missouri. Those years were all very exciting and stimulating for me. I learned a great deal.

Thirty-two years ago, I was asked to come to Jacksonville to be a faculty member at the University of Florida. I was to teach pediatrics and also work as a pediatric doctor in the Wolfson Children's Hospital in Jacksonville, a not-for-profit hospital that treats all children regardless of their ability to pay.

I am married and have two sons. My wife is a pathologist in a private practice. My two sons were born in the United States and have attended excellent schools and have great jobs.

Both my sons attended The Bolles School in Jacksonville and went on to attend Davidson College in North Carolina. My oldest son attended Harvard Kennedy School. He is now working in the U.S. State Department.

My younger son studied at LECOM and is a medical doctor in training at the University of Florida College of Medicine in Jacksonville Florida.

On the whole, my family and I have been positively treated as Muslims in the United States. Oh, there were the usual problems of being "randomly, chosen" to be inspected at security areas of airports. I'm accustomed to it and don't let myself get bothered by it.

After the events of 9/11, of course, there were some problems for my family, but we were fortunate to be helped to cope with them in surprising ways.

For example, I'll never forget when I called my oldest son's school shortly after the attacks on 9/11 and asked the principal if I should pick up my son immediately after the airplanes crashed into the World Trade Center. I was concerned about what might happen to him because of the anger that was being expressed by people after that tragedy. The headmaster told me that he would prefer my not picking up my son from school that day. He felt such an act would defeat the school's purpose of being a receptive school open to people of all faiths – even when one faith was being criticized and attacked. So, we left him stay in the school, and he did well.

The following year at the time of 9/11 commemorations, students were asked to write about the experience. My son's essay was selected as the best essay and he was asked to read it in front of the whole school.

My other son was playing basketball at the YMCA one day when another boy came up to him and hit him very hard and made some nasty remarks about him being a Muslim. My son wasn't injured badly. But he was shocked and saddened. I found out about this incident after my son had left for college when I read the essay in the school newspaper.

Perhaps one of the most difficult moments for me was when I was sitting in the physicians' lounge at the hospital and saw the second plane hit the World Trade Center towers. Another physician in the lounge shouted out: "Let's bomb the heck out of those Muslims." I found that very distressing and heartbreaking.

However, we had many supportive neighbors and friends, who made sure we were OK. They often came to our house, ringing our doorbell, and asking if there was anything we needed. One was the well-known banker Hugh Jones, who came by and said, "If there's anything you need, please call on me." I remember some of the Jacksonville leadership Class of 2003 folks, including an under-sheriff and Executive Officer of the Naval Air Station in Jacksonville, who reached out to me to assure me of their support. To me, it was like

43

seeing the glass more than half full.

I often say that after 9/11, 85% of the people who didn't personally know any Muslims would say, "Those Muslims are bad people." But of the people who knew a Muslim person, 95% of them said, "Muslims are good people." I believe it really often comes back to fundamentalism, which is a dangerous thing in any faith or religion.

After 9/11, I was often invited by different groups – churches, businesses, and civic groups here in Northeast Florida – to speak about what it's like to be a Muslim in the United States. I always talked about how we can make our country better if we contribute to its work.

I have faith that things will always get better, but I know we need to be involved to make that happen. It's not enough to just give money to a charity to help immigrants or people in need. We have to be involved.

Some of my special mentors have been Jews and Hindus. And when I was in a fellowship training at St. Louis, my office-mates were a Roman Catholic Christian and an Orthodox Jew from Israel. We worked in very tight quarters, but we became friends and worked well together and cared for each other.

My advice to everyone is get to know someone of another faith, and don't be afraid to do that. Try not to make any assumptions. When you know someone of another faith, you will have a better feeling about their faith or their religion.

I also encourage people not to try to learn about people of other faiths or customs or cultures from the media. Unfortunately, the media often shows the bad side of people rather than the good.

It's my strong belief that we do have more in common with each other than we have differences. I also suggest to people that they look for the things that they share with someone. And it's really important to look for the good in someone.

There are many people who feel that just by giving contributions to some kind of a charity is adequate. It's really not enough. Get involved.

DEAN JAMES PARKS MORTON

Respect for the Diversity of God's Kingdom
Former Dean of St John the Divine and
Director of the Interfaith Center of NY

My brothers and sisters, we are already one.
What we have to become is what we already are!
– Thomas Merton

There are some people who seem destined to make enormous changes and advances in opening the world to new ideas and opportunities. The Very Reverend James Parks Morton, who was the dean of the Cathedral Church of St. John the Divine in New York City for 25 years and founder of the Interfaith Center of New York, was such a person. He transformed many people's attitudes from almost static, judgmental positions into vibrant and lively interfaith and intercultural mindsets.

St. John the Divine, the seat of the Episcopal Diocese of New York, is said to be the largest Gothic cathedral in the world. In 1972, James Parks Morton was appointed dean of the Cathedral by the Rev. Paul Moore, Jr., the bishop of the diocese.

At the time, New York City was in the midst of a financial crisis, and the Cathedral appeared to be a symbol of the city's sluggishness. A century after its cornerstone had been laid, the building was unfinished. Much of the building and property were largely unused and neglected. Under Dean Morton's leadership, that picture would change drastically. He dreamed and worked for the church to involve the city in new and meaningful ways with social justice and interfaith programs.

In 1996, after 25 years of meaningful leadership, Dean Morton stepped down as dean of the Cathedral and immediately founded the Interfaith Center of New York. The Center focused on increasing respect and mutual understanding among people of different faith, ethnic, and cultural traditions and fostering cooperation among religious communities and civic organizations.

Since then, the Center has presented the James Parks Morton Award to religious leaders like the Dalai Lama and Imam Feisal Abdul Rauf and writers such as Bill Moyers and Nick Kristof. The award honors people who are "bold and courageous" – much like Dean Morton himself.

As can be seen in his story, Dean James Parks Morton thought big. He rarely did things on a small scale. He touched many lives.

Dean Morton's Story

In 1969 Paul Moore was elected Bishop Coadjutor of New York. The next year he asked me to consider being dean of the Cathedral of St. John the Divine. "The Cathedral has not had a dean since 1966," he said, "and it really needs to be turned around, and I think you're crazy enough to do it."

I took Paul's words seriously. I spoke at length with my wife Pamela and with dear friends as well, and they all said, "Go!"

So, in July 1972, Pamela and I, our four daughters, a green parrot, and a lemon tree arrived at the vast Gothic cathedral in a beat-up, rusty green Peugeot and moved into the 17-room stone deanery.

I spent my first day wandering the 13-acre close and looking at my new church. The structure was longer than two football fields and wide enough for a four-lane highway. And I was looking at a big, dark, empty place.

I vowed to start building the Cathedral again and fill it with activity, life, and light. We would use its big scale to move even a city as large as New York to action, healing, and communion.

But to make St. John the Divine become a reality in the modern city of New York, several changes had to be made. Global cities are full of immigrants from everywhere, of every language, religion, ethnicity, and culture. This would be a real challenge for the Cathedral, even with its inclusive 1873 charter declaring it to be a house of prayer for all peoples. How could a 20th century Episcopal Cathedral embrace the global diversity of New York City?

The providential jumpstart toward proclaiming and demonstrating the Cathedral's commitment to openness and diversity came in 1974 with a joint request from the United Nations and the Temple of Understanding that the Cathedral host and co-sponsor the celebration of the 30th anniversary of the founding of the United Nations in 1945.

The Temple of Understanding (America's oldest interfaith organization) was founded in 1960 by Juliet Hollister, the wife of a Wall Street banker. She was shocked that the nation's capital, among its great monuments to art, literature, and science, had no memorial to the deep wisdom and spiritual understanding of the world's great religions. The organization got its start not only with the public support of Eleanor Roosevelt but of 12 world-famous "founding friends" including Pope John XXII, Mother Teresa, Thomas Merton, the Dalai Lama, U Thant, Albert Schweitzer, Anwar Al-Sadat, and Jawaharlal Nehru.

The program for the anniversary Spiritual Summit Five Event, organized by the United Nations and the Temple of Understanding, began with an evening address from the Cathedral's pulpit by the anthropologist Margaret Mead, followed by prophecies chanted by Native American leaders, Muslim whirling dervishes, and Sufi circle dancing, which, to many people's surprise, almost everyone (including me) joined in!

The high point of the evening was the address by Juliet Hollister, who quoted Thomas Merton, the Roman Catholic monk: "My brothers and sisters, we are already one. What we have to become is what we already are!" Thomas Merton's words in the Cathedral that night became the theological rock of my life.

That event ended on Friday morning in the Dag Hammarskjold Auditorium at the United Nations with prayers by Mother Teresa, Hindu leader Sri Chinmoy, Rabbi Wolfe Kelman, Imam Pir Vilayat Khan, and Benedictine monk Brother David Steindl-Rast, with a final address by U.N. Secretary General Kurt Waldheim.

However, such interfaith diversity events have seldom been met with enthusiasm by all parties. In 1975, when some clergy in the diocese saw the photo in *The New York Times* of two Shinto priests with *Mikado*-like headgear in the pulpit – along with Margaret Mead and me as Dean – there were ominous rumblings.

Fortunately, the storm passed over, but it long remained a flickering red light for me.

Several positive and unexpected responses to that 1975 event brought the Cathedral of St. John the Divine into a new relationship with leaders at the United Nations, the American Muslim community, and Oomoto. The first of these meetings was with U.N. Secretary General Kurt Waldheim and resulted in the creation of the annual United Nations Sunday, which celebrates the September opening of the United Nations General Assembly. The newly elected assembly president preaches from the great pulpit of the Cathedral on the Sunday following that opening.

One day near Christmas, I received a call from U.N. Secretary General Kurt Waldheim regarding the visit to the Cathedral of the mayors of Bethlehem and Nablus and two others. Members of the PLO would also accompany them. So, four Palestinian mayors and their bodyguards were at my family's tree-trimming party that Christmas. As an old family tradition, we celebrated Christmas ecumenically as a feast of faith but also as a time of friendship. The Palestinians had stumbled onto this time with us.

Later we all trooped through the snow into the vast Cathedral for midnight Mass. And as is customary on solemn Cathedral occasions, a rabbi chanted the Old Testament lesson in Hebrew. The Arab mayors and the PLO looked on as "For unto us a child is born, for unto us a son is given," was read. The mayors knew better than most what the words were saying.

Then something happened that I never expected. The mayor of Bethlehem stood right up to Rabbi Gelber, grabbed him in a firm embrace, and kissed him on both cheeks. A sigh of delight from 4,000 people floated in the air. I hadn't been aware of it, but everyone was relieved. Their open hearts opened ours. At the conclusion of the service, Bishop Moore acknowledged the moment. "What we have all witnessed tonight," he said, "is the spirit that lies behind the United Nations – God's ever-creative spirit that unites us all."

This, I thought to myself, is what a cathedral is for.

Over the years, we honored St. John's Anglican heritage at the Cathedral, but at the same time we also welcomed the world's most creative spiritual leaders of different traditions as members of God's one family. The Cathedral became home to vast numbers of virtually all the world's many different religions.

The spiritual treasures of Islam, Buddhism, Japanese, and Native American traditions all became important dimensions of my own personal interfaith life. Also, I wear the black bear's tooth necklace around my neck instead of a gold or silver cross. The necklace was a gift from my interfaith pal, Tulley Spotted Eagle Boy, medicine man of the Micmac nation of Eastern Canada. Tulley became a Cathedral interfaith honorary canon. On Sundays, he would often join me at the altar. After I gave the sacred bread and wine to communicants,

Tulley would gently bless each person with his sacred eagle feather, reminding us of our deep connection to the earth.

When I was about to retire from the Cathedral in 1997, my friend Alan Slifka, president of the Big Apple Circus and my first Jewish trustee at the Cathedral, said to me: "New York, more than any city in the world, needs an interfaith center. After your 25 years at the Cathedral, you could do it."

Certainly, my years at the Cathedral with many of the world's most interesting religious leaders of different faiths, United Nations officials, environmentalists, and artists-in-residence, combined with my years of community-organizing in Jersey City and Chicago, all served as useful preparation for the Interfaith Center's operation.

The mission statement of the Interfaith Center of New York stated:

> The Interfaith Center of New York seeks to make New York City in the world safe for religious differences by increasing respect and mutual understanding among people of different faith, ethnic, and cultural traditions and by fostering cooperation among religious communities and civic organizations to solve common social problems.

When the Interfaith Center opened its doors in January 1997, globalization was a relatively new word. It underscores the planetary context of diversity itself in which many forms of differences in race, language, government, and religion co-exist. We must learn to live peacefully and with respect for the diversity throughout God's creation. But diversity in religion often seems difficult to understand.

In February 1997, the new Center held its first public program, "The Poor Are Credible," with an address by Muhammad Yunus, founder of Bangladesh's Grameen Bank – the world's first micro finance institution.

Beginning in 1998, our small paid program staff, together

with consultants and seminary interns, launched an intensive three-day-a-week schedule of visiting and personally getting to know the major religious leaders of the vast communities of recently arrived immigrants, new communities of Muslim, Buddhist, Hindu, Sikh, and Afro-Caribbean congregations which were located predominantly in the Bronx, Harlem, Brooklyn, and Queens. Our staff soon recognized the unique resource of the religious leadership which the new immigrant communities could become – if we created programs that were important both to them and to the secular leaders of the city of New York.

A large grant was given to the Interfaith Center in 1998 for a program of retreats on social justice and interfaith partnerships. The first retreat brought together 85 religious leaders and was focused on the subjects of immigration and police brutality. Since then, the retreats have provided opportunities for over 1,000 local New York grassroots religious leaders of diverse faith to develop strategies for addressing common social justice concerns and to build support networks.

The events of 9/11 represented a dramatic wake-up call for America and, indeed, for the world. Overnight, the word "interfaith" had taken on fresh meaning, and by 2000 the term itself had entered many people's vocabulary for the first time. The name and the work of the Interfaith Center was brought into the daily world of many organizations and newspaper readers throughout the country by the events of 9/11. Because of the response to its new recognition, the Center began seriously collaborating with major civic institutions from both New York City and New York State.

We must learn to live peacefully and with respect for the diversity throughout God's creation. Diversity is God-given.

* NOTE: Parts of this chapter are adapted with permission from James Parks Morton's memoir, With Companions for the Journey.

PRACHI RATHI

Living Peacefully and Harmoniously

A Hospitable & Peace-loving Hindu

I am a Hindu because it is Hinduism which makes the world worth living. I am a Hindu hence I love not only human beings, but all living beings.
--Mahatma Gandhi

Hinduism has long been recognized as a religion and a universal way of life. Its followers are to practice living peacefully and harmoniously in the world. As one of the oldest religions in the world that is still practiced, it does not have a founder, nor an organized clerical institution, nor an imposed dogma. Hinduism is the world's third-largest religion, with over 1.2-1.3 billion followers, or 15-16% of the global population. Many Hindus refer to their religion as Sanātana Dharma, which refers to the idea that its origins lie beyond human history. The teachings of Hinduism are also translated as an eternal and natural way to live.

In India, Hinduism is often seen as a way of life, a set of beliefs and practices spelling out right behavior and social order. One of the characteristics of Hinduism is that it recognizes that any person can have a personal concept and relationship with God, since God can have many forms. Thus, there are many representations of the Divine. At the core of Hinduism is pure love for God and genuine compassion for all beings.

According to Sri Aurobindo, "India is the meeting place of religions and Hinduism is vast and complex. Yet, it is more than a religion. It is a great diversified and yet unified mass of spiritual thought, realization and aspiration."

Prachi Rathi, her husband Manish, and their two beautiful daughters, Isha and Shailee, are devout, peace-loving Hindus. Their compassion and hospitality are exceptional. They strongly believe that people of all faiths and cultures are "good people" and that they should be treated with dignity and respect. And as can be seen in Prachi's story, they practice what they believe.

Prachi's Story

I was born in Nagpur, India in 1971. Both of my parents were wonderful people. They were devout Hindus – always loving their neighbors and their God. They were honest and had huge hearts. My mom and my dad were also great pray-ers, and I followed their lead. I have always felt blessed to have such parents.

I am a polio survivor. Although my mom was not highly educated, she was a brilliant woman. She was resilient, and she never gave up. She could see that when I was only one year old, I was not walking properly. She insisted that I be tested by a doctor. Although she was helping at a wedding, she came back from the wedding to take me by train to a doctor who had volunteered to see me. The doctor confirmed my mother's suspicions.

My treatment was to lie on a hard service, and my mom put heavy heat packs on the joints of my legs. It was a tough thing for both of us to do, but we did it. Today I am grateful that I do not have serious troubles from the polio. The only leftover problem is that there are some muscles on my legs that are not well developed.

Shortly after my illness, my mom became extremely sick with food poisoning and almost died. But somehow, she survived. Shortly after that, my dad developed tuberculosis. So, those years were difficult times for my family.

As I was growing up and attending school, I had both Hindu and Muslim teachers. They seemed the same to me. And I always had a special Muslim friend. We knew each other from kindergarten all the way through college, and we were like two peas in a pod. We both were high achievers and had strong study habits – even studying together in college. As best friends, we worked hard to help people see the importance of equality.

I decided to study Occupational Therapy at the University of Nagpur. In a way, I feel God helped me to make that decision. While at the University, I met my husband Manish, who was studying electrical engineering. We both were from the town of Nagpur. We had a nine-year courtship before we finally married in 1995.

After my graduation in 1986 from the Government Medical College of Nagpur, I had a degree in Occupational Therapy. I decided to further my studies in Mumbai (formerly Bombay). While standing in line waiting to pay my fees for my next studies in Mumbai, a woman in the line spoke with me telling me she knew a recruiter who helps people get work in America. Without much thought, I left the line to go to talk with this person. She also shared information about person who offered me a job in Mumbai with the Association for the Welfare of the Mentally Handicapped (AWMH). And from that meeting, I got referred to another part-time job at an orphanage, and I ended up being hired to work at both an orphanage and at the AWMH.

While working in Mumbai, I lived in a working women's hostel, where I was very fortunate to share a room with a blind woman. She was the editor of a Braille publication, and she was an amazing woman. I learned so much from her about living, being patient, and being kind. I will always remember my times with her.

In 1994, I had a call from the U.S. offering me a job as an

occupational therapist in Winter Haven, Florida. I accepted it, within a few months I got my work visa and flew to Tampa, Florida. When my plane landed in Tampa, it was the time when the Gator Bowl was about to happen. As a 22½ year old Indian woman, I had no idea why everyone was acting so strangely. I felt totally surprised.

When I first started living in Florida, I had some rather interesting experiences, which I can now laugh at. For example, I remember trying frantically to light an electric stove with a match. Also, it was difficult for me to understand the value of the American dollar as compared to the Indian rupee. I remember giving a taxi driver a $100 bill, and he didn't have enough change to give me. I thought $100 was the same as 100 rupees. The driver was very kind and understanding and we made an agreement that he would drive me at various times until I had used up the $100 worth of driving. I completely trusted him, and he didn't cheat me. And later when I first drove a car, I had no idea how to put gas in the tank.

Looking back, I now realize I was an Indian woman in a completely new environment. But I was so fortunate that people were very kind and understanding to me helping me to adjust to this new life. They did not do harm to me.

After six months working as an occupational therapist in Winter Haven, I was able to get my Professional License from Board of Occupational Therapy. And by January 1995, I had several job offers and eventually became a citizen of the U.S. in 2013.

My husband Manish and I had been married in India, and he was able to join me in Jacksonville, Florida. At that time there was a boom of IT work, and Manish was highly eligible for those jobs – having been trained in that field and as an electrical engineer.

We have two lovely, brilliant daughters who were born here in Florida: Isha, who is studying to be a Doctor of Osteopathic Medicine and who is now doing residency in family medicine, and Shailee, who is a psychology major at the University of Florida and is thinking of studying anesthesia. My daughters have never experienced discrimination and have been very much accepted.

Over the years, my personal experiences with Americans of all faiths have always been positive. I have never felt any forms of discrimination against me or my work. In fact, both my husband and I have always felt accepted and loved here.

We had only one uncomfortable situation in south central Florida when we stopped at a gas station. A man, who was obviously inebriated, came up to Manish and said: "Go back to your country."

As Indians and Hindus, we strongly believe in being peaceful. India has never started a war on its own. As Hindus, we also feel that atrocities and bullying should not be practiced nor accepted. If we see people who are practicing negative karma, we need to help them correct themselves.

Our faith is very important to us as a family. Every summer, we send our daughters to training camps to learn more about our Hindu faith. Because of that training, Isha and Shailee can lead our family in religious services on special holidays like Diwali (the Indian "festival of lights" which celebrates the triumph of good over evil and light over dark).

I personally believe that India is a very spiritual culture. People travel to India to ashrams and to be with people who pray, to see plants and animals living in harmony. For us, we can see God in every form.

Most people in the world are good people, who also want to live in peace. Of course, people will get offended if you talk offensively to them. Like my mom would say, we need to be resilient, to never give up, to be faithful, to love God and our neighbors, and to be big hearted.

SANDY HATCH

Letting Her Light Shine

Life in Mongolia

*As we let our own light shine, we unconsciously give other people per-
mission to do the same. No one is born hating another person because
of the color of his skin, or his background, or his religion.
Love comes more naturally to the human heart than its opposite.*
– Nelson Mandela

Mongolia!! When hearing that word, many people might say
"Where is Mongolia?" or "Who would ever choose to work
there?" or "Is there anything special there?" Mongolia sounds
cold and desolate, an extremely different place, and oh, so far
away.

In reality, Mongolia is a fascinating place with a very interesting history. Genghis Khan, a 13th-century warrior in central
Asia, founded the Mongol Empire, the largest empire in history with a vast amount of territory in China and central Asia.

The climate of Mongolia is harsh with very little rainfall and
wide seasonal temperature variations. Winters are long and
bitterly cold, and summers are short but pleasant. As the
world's largest landlocked country, Mongolia is also the most
sparsely populated country in the world with a population
of about 3.3 million. Much of its area is covered by grassy
steppe, with mountains to the north and west and the Gobi
Desert to the south. Ulaanbaatar, the capital and largest
city, is home to roughly half of the country's population.

Until the mid-20th century, the majority of the people led livestock-herding, nomadic lives. The herders are vulnerable to harsh natural conditions on the steppes. Some years, their herds are decimated by severe winters that ruin herders' livelihoods.

More recently, rural Mongolians are migrating to the cities. Many are unwilling to give up their traditional dwellings – round tents called *gers*, that are easily moved and provide shelter against the harsh winters. Communities of *gers* sprawl around major urban centers, but they lack full access to water and sanitation or to heating utilities. Thus, they rely on stoves, a source of pollution. Ulaanbaatar is one of the most polluted cities in the world.

And in this scene lived the lovely woman, Sandy Geiger Hatch, who had planned to work in South America and never dreamed of going to Mongolia. While serving on a one-year teaching assignment there, she enjoyed and loved the country and its people so much that she stayed and worked in Mongolia for 14 years – the longest of any American at that time.

Sandy's Story

Almost by accident, my husband Pete and I went to work in Mongolia in 1991. We didn't plan this, and I would never have imagined we would go there. We knew nothing about the country.

When I was growing up in Western Pennsylvania, there was a board on the wall in my church that had a panel of lights showing where different people were working around the world. As I looked at those lights, I felt sad that there were almost no lights in South America. So, as a child I started dreaming that I would go to work in South America. I wanted to be a "little light" there.

When I attended Eastern Baptist College, I studied Spanish. I was still hoping I would be on my way to South America. But unfortunately, the professor who taught Spanish left and was not replaced. Therefore, I changed my major to secondary education with a minor in English and history.

I met my husband Pete Geiger at Eastern College. He was a working journalist in the town of New Castle, Ohio. He was part of a team that won a Pulitzer Prize for their breaking story regarding the attempted takeover of Goodyear. I was very proud of him.

After graduation, I taught special education, pre-school, and kindergarten before becoming an activity director at a retirement community in Akron, Ohio.

A few years later, Pete was teaching journalism at Malone College in Canton, Ohio. One day he saw a flyer about a weekend retreat to recruit students to teach English as a second language in different places around the world. Pete and I talked about the retreat and decided it would be a fun thing to attend. We would have the opportunity to hear about different countries, and we thought that would be interesting. So, we went and enjoyed the buffet meals.

At our table, a young couple who were working in Mongolia told us a story about how caring and appreciative the people were of anything they did for them. I'll never forget the story they shared with us. Their students brought them a gift of gratitude. It was a basket full of cow dung. She explained to us that this was truly a special gift, because cow dung is precious and is carefully collected every day to use as fuel for cooking food and to heat peoples' homes – the round ger tents. The students had spent hours in minus 40-degree weather collecting dung for their teachers who had a ger stove in their apartment and thus would not be cold.

We were both deeply moved by that story – how although the people were very poor there, yet they were generous and big-hearted. As we drove home, we both knew we wanted to work there.

At first, we thought we might go for the minimum time of

three months. Then we realized it would be better if we stayed for a full year. So, we signed up for one year. To pay for the trip to Mongolia as well as all of our living costs, we had to raise our own funds. And we would not receive a salary.

I asked for a one-year leave of absence from my job as the activity director at the retirement community in Akron. Since Pete was working independently at the time, he could also take off for a full year.

We both went to Mongolia as teachers/professors at the college in Zuunmod, which is the capital of the state of Tov Aimag. Ulaanbaator – which means red hero – is the largest city and the capital of Mongolia.

Buddhism is the majority religion – although it is not much actively practiced. Non-religious are the second-largest group. When the Russians came to Mongolia, they tried to eliminate Buddhism by killing 400 Buddhist monks and burying them in a mass grave in our town. So, people of the younger generation mainly know Buddhism from the stories they were told. People also practice animism, and there are witch doctors. There was even a tiny church in Zuunmod, and the pastor was the ice hockey hero.

Pete and I felt comfortable with all the people. It didn't really matter to us what their practice of faith was or what they believed. They were people that we enjoyed and learned to love.

There were about 5,000 people living in our town of Zuunmod. It was called "the town of a hundred trees." One day, I walked around the town looking for the trees, and I did find more than 100 trees. However, they were only about as tall as I was.

In the summertime almost 60 percent of the people would leave the town to herd their animals (goats, cows, sheep, camels, yaks, horses). Often it was dangerous being herders, because there are many wild animals that stalked the herds. In the winter it was too cold to herd the animals, so the people returned to the town to live. At times, the temperature in the winter would get as low as -50°. Thus, from mid-October to mid-April the ground was frozen solid.

It's difficult for people to understand what it's like to live in Mongolia. For me, Mongolia is a land of two-humped camels; wild herds of antelope; packs of wild dogs, wolves, and Siberian tigers in the far-off mountains; and sheep as far as the eye can see.

Mutton was the meat of choice. And for supper, it was always *buuz* (steamed mutton dumplings) or *hoshur* (a mutton patty encased in a light layer of dough and fried in mutton fat, of course) – Mongolia's answer to a hamburger.

Approximately 30 percent of the population in the country is nomadic or semi-nomadic. They herd different kinds of animals – any kind that can be herded, so that doesn't include chickens.

Pete and I lived in a Russian-built apartment building. In our apartment, we had a kitchen, living room, bedroom, toilet room, and a sink and tub room. We even had a Russian washing machine and running water. The water and electricity would get turned off on a regular basis.

The winter months in Mongolia were brutal. The temperature in our apartment could get as high as 50°. That was about it. We just got used to wearing layers of clothes – several pairs of socks, long johns, sweaters, and coats.

Sometimes when it would get terribly cold, and we wanted to go outside of our apartment, we couldn't get our door open to the hallway. The hallways were frozen solid with ice and snow. It was a challenge, but we got accustomed to the cold weather.

There were only a few foreigners who lived in our town at that time. Many of the people surrounding our town lived in *gers*, which are a kind of round tent with an opening at the top for the smoke to get out. These "houses" were warmer than our Russian-style cement block apartment and were easy for the people to take down and move around – especially when they herded their animals during the summer months. For fuel for their stoves, the women collected dung from the animals every day, carrying baskets on their backs and flipping the dung into them.

Summers were quite beautiful there, but that was the time when we weren't teaching in the university. Many of the students went with their families to do herding. And Pete and I left during those months to return to the States to raise money, since we had to raise our own money to work and live there. We also raised money for scholarships for our students and for the poor children in the children's kindergarten.

In the town of Zuunmod, there was one large building that had shops where you could buy food. My students didn't want me to shop without their help, so they often accompanied me and carried the bags to my apartment up four flights of stairs.

We always walked to work at the university, which was about a half mile away. We didn't have a car, and there was no public transportation. Pete and I taught conversational English for three hours a day, four mornings a week. We also taught afternoon classes and evening community classes. My subjects included American Culture, Public Speaking, and International Etiquette. I also organized and supervised student teaching in the local elementary and secondary schools.

Our students ranged in age from 16 to 36. Students only went as far as the tenth grade before going to college.

The first year we taught there, we only had a few people in our classes. I believe I had 15 students. The second year we had more students. Every year it grew and grew. The students enjoyed coming to our home and often eating dinner with us in the evenings. In our last years working there, almost every night there was a group of students in our apartment sharing our dinner with us.

When I first got to Mongolia, I learned how much Mongolians loved chocolate. So, I decided that I would make some chocolate brownies for my students. At that time, I was not familiar with the stove we had in our apartment. I just assumed it would work the same way as my stove worked back in the United States.

When I thought the brownies were done, I took them out of the oven. They were hard as rocks – in fact they resembled *aruul*, which is a milk product Mongolians make and dry in sheets on the top of their *gers*. And they are as hard as rocks, so they break them into chunks. In fact, Mongolian mothers use chunks of one of these *aruuls* for teething purposes for their babies.

I was appalled that my brownies were ruined. However, I remembered that Mongolians had never eaten brownies before, so I served them to my students. They assumed I had made them to be this way. They gnawed away, ate every bit of them, and enjoyed them. But I never made brownies that way again. I learned to watch them carefully so they didn't turn out to be like rocks.

I have to laugh when I think that I never wanted to work in China or that I was only willing to work for one year. We ended up loving being teachers at the College in Zuunmod. Our students were the most enjoyable young adults who became our friends. And we ended up being there much longer than we ever imagined we would – 14 years.

LOIS YOUNG

Adventurous Woman

Born in Burma, Land of Mystery and Beauty

*We may have different religions, different languages,
different-colored skin, but we all belong to one human race.*
- Kofi Annan

Myanmar (formerly known as Burma) is a land of mystery and beauty. This beguiling country still retains an exotic allure. The country is diverse with roughly 135 ethnic groups. Myanmar is the largest country in Southeast Asia, with an area of almost 262,000 square miles. Myanmar has about 55.5 million people.

About 89 percent of the population of Myanmar are Theravada Buddhists. Most Burmese are very devout and treat one another with respect. Religious practice is not controlled by the government. Therefore, minority religious can exist openly, including Islam, Christianity, Animism, and tiny groups of Hindus, Taoists, and Mahayana Buddhists.

People have lived in Myanmar for at least 15,000 years. At one time, Burma was the richest country in Southeast Asia, full of jade, rubies, oil, and valuable timber.

The thick, unspoiled jungles of the country are home to many animals including elephants, tigers, and leopards, as well as

28 species of turtles and tortoises, and more than 1,000 kinds of birds.

In 2011, numerous political reforms took place in the country. After nearly 49 years, the first non-interim civilian president was elected. Unfortunately, Myanmar has become one of the poorest nations in the world. Per capita income is estimated to be about U.S. $230.

In this beautiful and exotic country, Lois Dickason Young was born in Rangoon in 1935. Living in this amazing land would have an enormous impact on her work, her values, her life.

Lois' Story

I consider myself a very fortunate woman. I was born to incredible parents at home on the campus of Judson College in Rangoon, Burma in 1935.

My father was Frederick Garrett Dickason. He was a professor at Judson College in Rangoon, where he taught zoology, botany, and other related topics. He seemed to know everything about bamboo, orchids, and ferns. These subjects were predominate in his mind and heart. At times I was able to travel with my father to look for new species of fern, bamboo, or orchids around the country. Travel was not easy at that time for anyone – my parents, local people, or myself. However, it was during these times that I learned most about the country, its flora, fauna, and other resources.

My mother Bertha was a nurse. She was an adventurer and could do everything. She was never afraid of anything. When I was quite young, she worked at a clinic on the back porch of our house. My sister and I helped care for babies and children in need of medical care, who lacked food and vitamins. They were undernourished and had serious skin difficulties. We had to wash their little bodies with gentian violet.

The babies often weighed two pounds or less, and sometimes they died in their mothers' arms. It was the job of my sister and me to line small boxes with my grandmother's linen napkins to prepare for the burial of these tiny babies. It was a wonder to work with these mothers and their weak but cherished babies, and both my sister and I became nurses after working with them.

My mother also worked in refugee camps. Often, she would have me accompany her. She had so much compassion. She tried to help people no matter what. I found that to be very inspirational.

During my early life, we lived in Burma during the Colonial Period in the political life of the country. It was a long period of colonialism under the political rule of the British. We lived on the Judson College campus in a colonial style house with about seven house staff to keep the big house working. We needed the staff, as we had little running water or refrigeration. Shopping needed to be done daily for food. Also, many sellers of produce would come to the house to sell us things. We always had very healthy food, fruits, and vegetables.

Our staff would collect water and heat it for bathing. One day when I was a young child, our bearer was carrying a very big tub of boiling hot water up the stairs for our baths. I was running around the house and ran right into the bearer, so the hot water poured over most of my body. I was deeply burned and blistered. It took years to heal those burns.

One of the people who came to take care of me and nurse me was the mother of Aung San Sun Kyi. She and my mother became close friends. Later, Aung San Sun Kyi became the politician and author who won the Nobel Peace Prize in 1991. At the time, she was still under house arrest for challenging the army generals who ruled. I met her a number of times.

Burma offered a multi-cultural society with Burmese plus approximately 15 other tribal groups, who had various cultural backgrounds and languages. We knew and cared for Buddhists as well as Hindus, Muslims, and Christians. Many of the professors at the college were good friends and colleagues of my father. I still have a feeling of love and joy in my heart as I remember them.

Most of our Burmese friends were from well-educated college families. One of our neighbors who lived in the compound with us was the Burmese president of the college. When we were young, I often played with his children. This dissipated somewhat when I went to boarding school in Woodstock in North India and later to Kodai School in South India. However, we rejoined as friends when we met up during our college years.

I was homeschooled until high school. British children usually returned to Britain after approximately age nine to attend boarding schools there, although there were good schools in Rangoon with well-trained Burmese teachers. However, it was not the custom for Western children to attend Burmese schools. British mothers parted from their children not knowing when they might see them again. This was very difficult for many families.

In 1943, during the Second World War, we were evacuated from Burma to India. We were very nervous when we got to the harbor in Rangoon. Our ship had sailed early to India due to a promised bombing of the harbor from the Japanese ships carrying torpedoes. The American Embassy sent cars and launch boats to help us reach our ship and sail to Calcutta. After long travel, we did reach our destination in India.

My dad stayed behind to help other people get evacuated, so my mom took us four children – my two older sisters, my younger brother David who was four, and me at seven.

When we reached Calcutta, we were to catch a train from Calcutta to Rawalpindi which is on the other side of India (now a part of Pakistan). My mother was trying to meet someone who was to help us get to Rawalpindi. That person did not show up, so my mom told us children to stay on the train and not to allow anyone to move the train until she came back. She needed to find this person. So, the four of us children were sitting on the train by ourselves, and we were concerned that the train would leave and we would never see our mother again. Every now and then the conductor would come in and ask us, "Has your mother returned?" And we would say, "No, not yet."

We could see the flagman outside the train who was still holding a red flag, and we were worried it was going to turn to green, and we would be lost. Finally, our mother returned, and we made the long trip across India to Rawalpindi.

I was young when we lived in Rawalpindi. I enjoyed my play time with village children there, who were mostly Indians. They were both Hindu and Muslim. They were often busy helping their mothers collect buffalo dung for fuel. But when we were together, we would play marbles, spin tops, or roll wheels. Often, we had our arms around each other's necks, and we would laugh. We even collected squirrels. It was a free and joyful time for me. Later, I went to Woodstock School high in the Himalayan Mountains. I remember it as being very beautiful.

My family returned to the U.S. in 1943. It was a 43-day trip on that boat because we went via New Zealand and Australia. We had to zigzag across the ocean for fear of being sunk by German torpedoes. We stayed in the U.S. until 1946 when we went back to Burma.

In 1953, I returned to the U.S. by myself on the ship USS President Cleveland. It was quite an interesting trip because President Truman was on board along with his wife Beth and daughter Margaret. I often walked the decks with President Truman, and I even danced with him one evening. He was delightful. No security then!

When I returned from overseas to the U.S., I went to Wooster College and then on to nursing school at Western Reserve University. As I matured, I got married in 1957 to Jack Young, a magnificent man, and we had a family. We moved to New York City where I worked as a visiting nurse in a poverty-stricken area in Harlem. I often worked with young girls who were pregnant. I walked the streets day and night, wherever I was called to go. I often climbed up five flights of stairs a day. The people were so kind to me, and I loved them.

Later I co-founded the Newgrange School for students who had learning difficulties. I also established a literacy program in the New Jersey maximum-security prisons. I then worked with others to develop The Cetana Educational Foundation in Burma, which taught English as a second language and established scholarships for Burmese students for entrance into colleges in Thailand and the U.S.

Now as I look back on my life, I realize it has been a great adventure. It has been a pleasure to get to know people of many backgrounds, faiths, and cultures that have had an enormous impact on my work and my life.

I was also blessed with a merry spirit, and I had my mother's adventurous soul. I was always interested and inspired by people of other backgrounds. I loved the Burmese, the Indians, the Sikhs. I have appreciated the Jewish peoples' customs and their humor, and the Buddhists' family life, values, and gentleness.

I guess I believe that Jesus would also have been moved by all those people. He would have loved everybody. He said, "Let the children come to me for of such is the Kingdom of God." Yes, I am a very fortunate woman who has lived an exciting and adventurous life.

Matt Hartley

Energy at the Intersections

Director of Interfaith Center, University of North Florida

God has given us many faiths but only one world in which to co-exist.
May our work help all of us cherish our commonalities
and feel enlarged by our differences.
– Lord Jonathan Sacks

In some sense, Matt Hartley, the director of the Interfaith Center at the University of North Florida, is not unique.

Matt was three weeks into his freshman year as a student at the University of North Florida on September 11, 2001. The terrors of that day and the following aftermath were both heartening and discouraging. Heartening to see people of the U.S.A. come together across many differences in order to support each other. Discouraging in that the togetherness, for many, required a common enemy which emerged as the Islamic faith.

Matt used that terrible day as a catalyst for the work he continues to do to this day. This interaction and others like it caused Matt to dive deeper into the Muslim experience in America and especially in the American South. His longing to have a more accurate picture of these events sent him to the University of Florida to pursue a master's degree in religion.

However, looking at Matt's story, one can see that the seeds of his beliefs and commitments were planted in some early and quite unexpected places.

Matt's Story

I was born the child of a minister. My father was a minister in the Christian Missionary Alliance, and my earliest memories are of growing up in the church parsonage in a small Indiana town.

Along the way, as any good Christian might do, I began to memorize portions of the Bible. One of the first verses I memorized was from the third chapter of John, verse 16, "For God so loved the world." It was in memorizing that particular text and considering God's love for the entire world that my life work began to take shape.

I saw the words of John 3:16 lived out in the career path of my father. He became a chaplain whose relationships transcended traditional Christian denominations and included people of different faith traditions.

I remember a special relationship between my father and a Jewish rabbi as particularly forming my understanding of interfaith friendship and cooperation. I also learned that just because two people or groups claim the same faith/denominational name does not mean the groups are uniform in their understanding or practice of their particular faith.

Then, as now, there is deep diversity within similar faith and denominational families. It takes focused attention, a discerning eye, and the passage of time in order to appreciate and name the diversity within those traditions.

My response to the 9/11 tragedy continued as I pursued a minor in religion. In particular, I was, and still am, interested in moving religious understanding from just an individual understanding to a collective appreciation of similarities and differences. I think of it as: "From mine [religion] to all [religions]."

Upon graduation my career took me as an educator to the

classrooms of Sandalwood High School in Jacksonville, Florida. There I had a firsthand look at the diversity which is public education in the United States. Given my past experience, I was especially interested in the large number of Muslim students who attended Sandalwood and were students in my classes. What was most surprising was the way Muslim students integrated into the larger Sandalwood community.

One day two of my students were having a conversation. One of the students was from the Islamic community and the other was not. I cringed when I heard one student stereotype Muslims by saying, "Aren't all of you terrorists?"

Instead of the Muslim student being angry, I was amazed at his ability to disarm prejudice. The 16-year-old Muslim student responded, "Aren't all you guys racist?"

This interaction and others like it caused me to dive deeper into the Muslim experience in America and especially in the American South. My desire to have a more accurate picture sent me to the University of Florida in pursuit of a master's degree in religion.

The education experience proved instructive for me. In researching the pillars of "American" Islam, I found that Muslim youth, by and large, are extremely gifted in practicing their faith in various communities around Florida. My research focused on the Jacksonville, Tampa, and Gainesville areas. I often heard that the American South was a "good place to be a Muslim" and a "good place to practice religion" – voiced by some of the religion's youngest practitioners.

Perhaps my hopes arising from the 9/11 tragedy were beginning to be realized.

While I was pursuing my master's degree, I was also actively serving a church which was part of the Presbyterian Church (U.S.A.). The service in the church was important to me and instructive for anyone pursuing work in interfaith spaces.

I realized that one does not need to give up the particularity of one's own tradition in order to appreciate and learn from others. As a matter of fact, time and again, folks who engage in interfaith friendships and dialogue come away with a deeper, greater, and more profound understanding of their own faith.

Interfaith friendship is good and doesn't "threaten" another's faith. The hope is that we can find each other in the midst of difference.

Despite many gains in interfaith cooperation, the work is still done by a small group of people. It is easy to fall into a "preaching to the choir" mindset, which gathers folks who already believe and practice this work.

In addition to the surprises I learned from Muslim youth, I have also been astonished by some of the unique places my work has taken me – none more so than a prominent evangelical church on the Southside of Jacksonville.

I was invited to convene an interfaith panel for the church's college group. Most who gathered in the room were unfamiliar with interfaith work or thought that interfaith work served to dilute one's previous commitment to faith.

To my surprise, an evening of listening and sharing provided a valuable, teachable moment. Many in the room walked away feeling hopeful regarding interfaith outreach and believing it bolstered, rather than threatened, their personal faith commitment. If it can happen there, maybe anywhere.

It is the hope of happening anywhere that leads me into this calling and vocation. I now serve as the director of the Interfaith Center at the University of North Florida. The center has continued to grow as one of the preeminent collegiate interfaith centers in the country. I believe the center's growth is directly related to its remarkable students.

I find "energy at the intersections" – the intersections where people of different faith commitments, understandings, and worldviews come together in order to make a "new normal." My hope for the future is a "new normal" founded on trans-formation, a future where the divisiveness and Islamophobia post-9/11 are things of the past.

STANLEY WAGNER

Being Part of the Culture

An American Boy Growing Up in an Indian Culture

While living the life of a wave, the wave also lives the life of water.
It would be sad if the wave did not know that it is water.
- Thich Nhat Hanh

Growing up and living life in several different cultures can be both stimulating and confusing. Often people feel they are a part of the culture that they are born and raised in, and therefore they understand the world in similar ways in which the people of the culture of their birth does. They learn to see things through the eyes of that culture with its subtleties. Their own perspective and insights about their family's heritage or culture may become disoriented, even temporarily lost.

For people born and raised in one country by parents who come from another place, their upbringing can feel like a kind of conglomerate of several worlds. They might want to identify with their parents' traditions, but feel that they are unable to do so because they are a part of their birth culture. They may even face criticism for behaving differently than what is normally acceptable in their parents' customs.

Sometimes, returning "home" to one's heritage culture after a long period of time may feel foreign and confusing. Adapting to this "new" environment can be complicated and alien to their cultural origins and learnings. The expressions of communication, the language, and the customs may initially feel challenging. That is especially true if the person experiences a sense of judgmentalism, bullying, or cliquishness when returning to that culture.

However, being bi-cultural can be tremendously beneficial and advantageous for those people who are able to navigate the streams of multiple cultures. Research has shown that people who are bi-cultural often are more open-minded, accepting, and creative in their thinking.

Certainly, that is the case for Stanley Wagner, a retired cardiologist, who was born in India of American parents and now lives in the U.S.

Stanley's Story

I was born March 14, 1941, in the town of Mussoorie, located in the cool hills of northern India. Mussoorie was one of several "hill stations" to which the elite British colonial government officials could escape to avoid the blistering heat of the tropical Indian summers. The town also had a language institute established primarily to instruct missionaries and others in the language of the region to which they were assigned to work.

In 1937, my parents went to India as Methodist missionaries. During the summers, they traveled to Mussoorie for a few months for language training. As a pastor, it was helpful for my dad, as he was able to listen and talk to people in their own language. During her late pregnancy, my mother went to Mussoorie to escape the heat of the plains. Thus, I was born there, one of four children.

My father was first assigned for three years to be the pastor at the Byculla Memorial Church in Bombay (Mumbai), a mostly English-speaking congregation. I have very few memories of living there. However, I do remember playing in our compound with my older brother and children of the church workers. We spoke Marathi to our playmates and English with our parents.

During World War II, we were evacuated back to the U.S. on a military troop ship. We sailed around the Cape of Good Hope in South Africa and zigzagged across the ocean to avoid torpedoes. When we got to the U.S., we went to my mother's home in Montgomery County, Maryland, where we had lots of relatives. I have very little recollection about how I felt about being there. I have some vague memories of being uncomfortable and people leaning over me and asking me to "speak some Indian," which I wouldn't do.

While we were in the U.S., when I was about four, my dad went to Hartford for some training for basic healthcare treatments. He knew that where he was assigned to work in rural Hyderabad State in India, health care needs were great. The training was focused on how to treat infections and what kinds of medications one might use in the villages.

When we returned to India, I was ready for school and went to boarding school in Mussoorie. My family moved to different places over the years, and I visited them in the winter months for three months when I wasn't in school.

From age five years to high school graduation at 17, my brothers and I would take a 1,500-mile, four-day train trip to Mussoorie to stay in a boarding hostel as part of Woodstock School, a missionary-supported school. The school had a strong reputation for excellence over its 100 years of service. Children attended from numerous nations, representing all religions from the Middle East countries to Korea, and included many children from India. Although loyal to its Christian roots, there was an emphasis on tolerance for all beliefs. We considered classmates as equals – equals to do good, and equals to get into trouble.

Many of my classmates started boarding school at an early age (five years). We missed our families, and we all experienced loneliness. However, that seemed a vulnerability, and none of us would express how we felt. We just cried into our pillows at night. Not expressing feelings of vulnerability or hurt would set a pattern that I would struggle with the rest of my life. On the positive side, we developed a resilient self-independence. The weekly letters from home that my mother sent, and her love and caring when we were together, formed the core of my concept of love.

Since the Woodstock School was located at 6,500 feet elevation in the forest and foothills of the Himalayan Mountains, we were surrounded by natural beauty. Throughout the school year, students and faculty would take three- to ten-day hikes into the hills. It seemed part of our curriculum, and certainly part of our lives.

Because the school was located at the eastern edge of Mussoorie, about once a month students would walk into town to "check it out." My favorite memories are going to a local street shop to have *dahl* (cooked lentils) and *puris* (a deep-fried tortilla) for about 10 cents U.S. currency – a week's allowance. The local sweet shop was also a favorite spot. Our interactions with townspeople were friendly and respectful as children to adults.

For nearly 25 years, my parents served very poor rural populations throughout northern Hyderabad State. They lived in five villages, usually on the edge of town. Whenever I was there, I played with my elder brother and the children of village families. We enjoyed flying kites, which we learned how to make from our Indian friends. We mixed crushed glass with sticky cactus juice and carefully coated the string nearest the kite. Then we joined the village kite fights, where each kite flyer would try to maneuver his kite to cut the string of his opponent's. Skill and fair play were the rules. So, during those days, I felt very much a part of an Indian child's life.

Every Christmas my parents and we children would crowd into a jeep to visit each of the local villages for Christmas celebrations. This included songs in Marathi, a slideshow on some aspect of public health, a Christmas service, and a dinner. Fifty to 100 villagers were able to purchase only one chicken, which was made into a fiercely spiced curry soup that served all. I was impressed that despite the abject poverty of the community, people would share what they had for their celebration.

The need for basic healthcare was great, and both my parents went to local villages to discuss and demonstrate public health practices. My parents also ran a twice-weekly dispensary out of the storeroom next to our home. The clinic was open to all, regardless of religion or social status. I saw many people with leprosy who had missing fingers or toes, hands or noses. My father cared for local infections and helped in getting people transferred to distant leprosariums. I believe it was that very basic healthcare clinic that stimulated me to one day become a doctor.

Although my dad went to India as a Christian missionary, his college degree was in civil engineering. He was not just a preacher and the superintendent of the regional conference; he was a jack of all trades. In India there was an urgent need for schools, hospitals, health dispensaries, roads, water wells, and churches. My dad became a construction supervisor for many building projects for the church in Hyderabad State. He helped to build a school system, the roads in nearby villages, even a well. He had demonstration plots of land showing the difference between using fertilizer or not.

At one point, my dad's life was in danger. It's difficult to know about stories from the past – if I remember them correctly. But I recall it this way. In 1947, there was a nationwide uprising of Muslims and Hindus against each other during the partition of India and Pakistan. Although Hyderabad State was considered to be a Muslim state, the population was 25 percent Muslim and 70 percent Hindu.

During partition, people were being killed and tortured. As time went on, people began to express anger at the English, who were blamed as the ones responsible for the mess throughout the country. It's not unusual for citizens of a new nation to feel powerful and angry. So, the people planned to kill those they didn't like – mainly the British people. One night my dad was returning home, and he came across a roadblock of angry Hindus. They told him they were going to hang him.

Fortunately, the Muslim superintendent of police, with whom my father had worked, came by at that moment and asked them what they were doing. "We are going to hang this Englishman." The Muslim superintendent knew my dad was an

American who had done many positive things for the people of the local district. He started asking the Hindus questions: "Did you know this man had this road built for you?" "And did you know that up the road where you get water from the wells, this man built those wells?" After a lot of talking, they finally let my dad go free.

That was a near miss. I was living in the hill country at school at the time, so I wasn't there when this happened. However, I felt a deep sense of sadness because many of the cooks for the Westerners were Muslims. They would handle meat when they cooked, which the Hindus would not do. There were bands of people coming around looking for Muslims to kill. Many of the Westerners and well-to-do Indians would hide, protect, or send their Muslim cooks away to safety. It was a terrible time. And the same thing was going on in Pakistan with the Muslims against the Hindus.

My dad told me that he wanted me to become a missionary. However, I knew I wanted to be a doctor – perhaps to work in a medical mission. I was confident it would be worthwhile as a career to help people out.

At age 17, I returned to the U.S. for college. I had always considered myself an "American," but with emotional and cultural ties to India. I grew up listening to many languages that were interesting, but not threatening. These cultural connections were contrasted when I returned to the U.S. In many ways, I felt a stranger to U.S. culture, particularly the teen culture. This took years to digest and adjust to, but I had my focus on becoming a doctor. Thus, college and post-graduate training were forefront in my life.

For years after my return, I decided that my youth in India was a past part of my life, and I tried to cut off my connections – except to Indian food, which was an emotional and gustatory necessity. This love was shared with my wife and children, who to this day demand we have Indian food when we have family reunions.

89

NAGAT KHALIFA

A Brilliant Student

Giving Authentic Witness to Her Islamic Faith

We aren't called to be a judge; we are called to be a witness.
— Stacy L. Sanchez

In the fall of 2018, Nagat Khalifa first became a student at the University of North Florida (UNF) studying Political Science. She was a first-generation college student in her Egyptian-American family.

In the spring of 2019, Nagat made the decision to start wearing the hijab. In modern usage, the hijab generally refers to various head coverings worn by Muslim women. It is a visible representation of being a devout Muslim. Unfortunately, the hijab can be used as a weapon to marginalize women through social and political misconceptions.

Over the months and years that Nagat Khalifa attended UNF, people came to appreciate and respect her for her work in advocacy for refugee women. They learned about her faith story, through her work with the Interfaith Center.

Her presence on the UNF campus had a positive impact on the work of the Interfaith Center – as well as on the entire UNF campus community, through her involvement with Student Government, the Honors College, and co-founding the Arab Student Union organization.

It is a pleasure to share Nagat Khalifa's story and her pride in being a Muslim woman.

Nagat Khalifa's Story

People often hear stories about how Muslim women are forced to wear the hijab, but I want to tell my story of why I adopted wearing the hijab and how it became central to my expression of faith.

Throughout my life, I've always been a person open to the experiences of other people. Since 2016, my mother and I have helped the refugee community, with emphasis on Muslim women and single mothers. I also spent time working with middle school students from first-generation and low-income backgrounds to encourage them to strive for a higher education.

My first real encounter with interfaith differences that I can remember happened when I was attending middle school, where there was a girl from Iraq. She was a first-generation American, and she wore a hijab to school. I remember that she was bullied for being Muslim. For some reason, I jumped into the conversation defending her, not knowing how or why I did that.

That encounter led me to start my journey on learning about my own religion. In learning about Islam, I have always focused on how it was similar to other religions rather than on the differences. As I concentrated on learning about my faith, I began to own my faith back from what society has said about Islam being an oppressive religion. But all along it was non-oppressive!

When I came to UNF, I was a part of the Quest Program which introduced me and others who were first-generation college students to important resources on campus. During my first months on campus, I met Matt Hartley, Director of the Interfaith Center at UNF.

Meeting Matt was a major turning point on my journey. He asked me to be a part of "The Better Together Team" – the student leadership group at the UNF Interfaith Center.

So here I was learning more about my own faith, while focusing on similarities and differences of faiths around the world. As I continued to explore my own faith, I began to wonder if perhaps I was ready to wear the hijab. I was slowly becoming more confident about my own faith identity, as I was involved in interfaith work.

I remember having a conversation with my mother who asked me if I knew why I wanted to wear the hijab. She wanted to test me on my true intentions, on whether I felt forced to wear it or if the decision happened of my own free will. Wearing the hijab is a commitment to God, and she did not want me to make light of it.

I knew it was important that I do my own research about this. I was always a questioning person. I wanted to find out reasons, answers, and thoughts regarding my faith.

On the other hand, my father was afraid of any questioning. He did not even allow reading a Bible one finds in hotel rooms. He feared that it might lead to conversion.

Eventually, with my interfaith work, I began to live past my father's influence and truly started learning about my identity.

Later, my mother married an Imam. I asked him all sorts of unanswered questions that I always had about Islam. "Does Islam oppress women?" "What are the rights that women have in the Islamic faith?" "What are some of the most important beliefs about our faith?"

As I continued my research, I learned many realities of my faith. At first, I thought wearing the hijab was a symbol of oppression, but as I progressed in my learning, I could see that it was not. It is an authentic expression of my own faith.

So, in the second semester of my freshman year on April 1, 2019, I began to wear the hijab. I woke up that cold morning, feeling God's presence. Without thinking, I grabbed a winter scarf and covered my head. I felt an emotional connection with God, and I was compelled to take the steps to confidently show my faith through wearing the hijab.

It wasn't long before I began to understand that oppression does not come from wearing the hijab, but rather it occurs when a culture or society endorses patriarchal traditions that oppress women, instead of trying to understand that Islam gives women many rights!

Soon, I connected with many Muslim women in Jacksonville through my work with the refugee community. After deciding to wear the hijab, I was able to understand better and join in on the shared hijabi experience with other Muslim women. I am very proud to publicly express my faith by wearing the hijab.

Towards the end of my studies at UNF, I wrote a paper for an international studies class about the factors that oppress Muslim women compared to what mainstream media has led western society to believe. It further confirmed what I was feeling and thinking about my faith. Soon after that, I began to see more of my friends start wearing the hijab, publicly expressing their faith.

I remember the first time I saw Minnesota Representative Ilhan Omar in Congress. She was wearing a hijab. It was a very empowering moment for Muslim women to see a Congresswoman wearing the hijab. It helped me to not be afraid about publicly wearing it.

I always felt that I was incredibly welcomed at UNF. I knew I could be completely who I was in my faith tradition, and that I would be accepted and loved by the community.

These days I now give my time working in Washington, D.C. for a non-profit organization that focuses heavily on diplomacy and international work.

I strongly believe that women of all faiths should have the right to make their own decisions concerning their lives. I have many dreams for the future including working with refugee women, being a leader in interfaith dialogues, and advocating on behalf of vulnerable people throughout the world.

ANNA

Sowing Tiny Seeds of Forgiveness

A Jew in a Nazi Concentration Camp

If you want to see the brave, look at those who can forgive.
If you want to see the heroic, look at those
who can love in return for hatred.
– Bhagavad-Gita

Sometimes our interactions with people of other cultures, faiths, or backgrounds can be painful – even life-threatening.

Anna is someone who found herself in such a situation. She was a Jewish woman born in Hungary. When the ethnic cleansing began, and Jewish citizens were forced to leave their homes, members of Anna's family suffered greatly. She and her family eventually became prisoners in a Nazi concentration camp in Germany. They experienced extreme loss, trauma, and distress.

For Anna and those who have experienced deep damage and pain, it's easy to fall into despair and grief. As victims of brutal treatment, the healing process can be a lifelong challenge.

For Anna, telling her story was a way of bringing her anguish out of the dark corners of her mind. It helped her to face her fears and release buried hurtful feelings. The wounds of her misery and suffering lost some of their lethal power when brought into the open within a meaningful context.

As Anna talks about feeling a sense of sadness and even empathy for her torturers and forgiving her enemy, she reminds everyone to remember that there is a world of refugees and people, whose roots are in countries that have been so-called "enemies." They, like Anna, are in need of healing from their pain or their shame.

As Anna shares her story, she no longer feels hatred toward her enemies. She finds herself feeling pity and a kind of compassion for them.

Anna's Story

I was born in Hungary before the start of the First World War. My family were pious and scholarly Jews.

When the Nazis came to power in Germany, we heard rumors about them. Life moved on without our recognizing the signs of disaster. On March 13, 1938, our destiny came crashing down when the Germans marched in. My family crawled into our apartment immobilized with fear. We were the only family in danger in our building. Our neighbors isolated us and asked us to understand.

Through years in Vienna, we kept our Hungarian passports. Now it was advantageous to be foreigners. The streets of Vienna were full of SA men (the original paramilitary wing of the Nazi party) who could take you away if you could not identify yourself as an Aryan or a foreigner.

Many people started looking for ways to emigrate, crowding in front of embassies to get visas. An American visa was favored, but difficult to obtain. We had no friends or relatives abroad and no means to buy visas.

My aunt begged us to go to Czechoslovakia to be safer. It was unthinkable something similar could happen there. We turned her invitation down. Not long after that, Hitler occupied the Czech Republic in 1939 and made it part of Germany. The ethnic cleansing began.

That year we moved to Budapest. Emil, a lawyer who wanted to marry me, received a visa to the U.S. He invited me to join him. In September 1939, I went to the American Embassy with documents from Emil to apply for a visa. The Embassy sent me an official confirmation letter stating I had applied for a visa. I kept that paper not knowing how important it would be.

In 1944 the Germans occupied Hungary, and suddenly Nazi signs were everywhere. As Jews, we felt trapped without any escape route. We didn't know who might be a Nazi agent – even concierges in apartment buildings.

As non-Aryans we had to wear the yellow star, and our apartment was marked. We were registered and under observation. Anyone who addressed a star-wearer in the street could also be registered. Families and friends were ripped apart. The death penalty was set for anyone who didn't respect the rules.

Then the bombing began. We went to our building's basement, sometimes waiting through the entire night in dark rooms.

One day the concierge said my sister and I were to report to a sports stadium. We knew that this meant we would be sent to a concentration camp. We spent several days at the stadium sleeping in the cold with almost no food or water.

We were told foreigners should identify themselves. We decided to claim we were Americans, using the English letter from the U.S. Embassy confirming my visa application. After checking our papers, we were sent to a schoolhouse with other foreigners.

Our mother arrived the next day, and we believed we were no longer in danger. We didn't know by coming there, our mother missed the chance to survive in the ghetto as some did.

One day in the school's courtyard, a "doctor" checked each person. My sister, mother, and I were put into the same group. Surrounded by Nazi troops, we were marched out of town on a long, miserable trek to a concentration camp.

We were hungry and thirsty and lost our energy and stamina. Our clothes got wet and heavy. Our shoes disintegrated, making every step painful. Those who could not walk fast were shot. My sister and I dragged our mother between us.

Finally exhausted, we reached a German city, where I thought we would be safe. Afterall, this was a nation of culture, the country of my admired author Goethe. As we passed Nazi officers, one called: "Lousy, filthy Jews."

We were shoved into cattle cars on a train. We had to stand or sit on the floor. The guards dumped moldy bread into our car and slammed the door shut.

When the doors opened, we were ordered off the train. Many people died during the trip. In such tight space, we hadn't noticed that someone next to us was dead.

As we marched through the streets, I saw a church and felt consoled that people who lived here went to church and knew the Christian commandments. They would not harm us.

Finally, we walked into Ravensbruck Concentration Camp. We registered as American citizens. After that, we received ragged clothes, which I never once changed in Ravensbruck. Then we went to "the block," where we slept in racks of wood stacked on top of each other. Three people slept in each rack like sardines with no covers or pillows.

Inspection started while still dark. Anyone who could not stand during inspection was sent to the "furnace." We could smell the putrid smoke.

After inspection we were given a piece of bread and heavy shovels. We marched to a work area where we shoveled hills of sand from one place to another. Every day, the routine was repeated.

Days passed and many did not survive. Everyone was afraid of diarrhea, caused by typhoid from polluted water. Often, we drank it because of our endless thirst.

The last winter of the war was extremely harsh. It was impossible for my mother to do hard work. She became ill from typhoid. She went to the revier for the sick. A few days later, she died. We felt grateful her difficulties had ended.

One morning I had a high fever, so I was sent to the revier. The only advantage was I could rest. Several days later, my sister came to the window saying, "You must leave immediately. The revier will be cleared out tonight." I didn't want to leave my bed, but my sister pulled me through the window and dragged me to our block. My sister saved my life, for that night the revier was emptied.

As the Allies got closer to our camp, the camp commanders began to hand out American Red Cross packages to the foreign prisoners. As "Americans," we were given a care package from the Red Cross. We rushed to our block and opened the box containing chocolate, sardines, raisins, dried milk powder. Unfortunately, these goodies proved harmful. We gulped down most of the chocolate and sardines and mixed the milk powder with contaminated water. We became violently ill.

Soon, a prisoner told me there were busses to take foreign prisoners to Sweden, and we should go to the gate. There stood the famous busses of Count Folke Bernadotte, the President of the Swedish Red Cross.

For the last time we stood for inspection as the camp commander instructed us not to take bad memories. His words were pathetic. Perhaps he realized that he would be held responsible by the world's judges and by his own conscience.

Many years later, my adult children surprised me with a special gift of "a weekend in a Catholic monastery" not far from Hamburg. Initially I was afraid to go. I might be driven away if they learned I was a Jew – not a Catholic. With a closed heart I went.

That experience launched a new life for me. The monks provided a "home" for people in need. I was received openly and lovingly. No one tried to convert or influence me.

As I reflect back on that dreadful time in history, I realize the atrocities that occurred could not have happened without the help of the wider world. Most governments were acquainted with the work of the Nazis. It was not a secret. Yet they stood by and watched without taking action, allowing millions of people to be killed.

Countries could have kept their borders open for refugees and welcomed them. People were often cheated for worthless visas. The institutional church also failed by remaining silent and pretending not to see. The whole world should be judged on this matter. Unfortunately, humankind has not learned much from this.

As time goes by, I think about the people who tortured and guarded us. I wonder how they dealt with their roles. Did they go home after work and behave as if they were tired from some kind of honest work? Were they able to play happily with their children, romance their wives or husbands, or walk the dog after they had heartlessly killed and cruelly hurt uncounted numbers of people? Did they go to church and pray the Lord's Prayer? Or did they feel no guilt because they thought they had merely extinguished unworthy lives?

As a victim it's important not to fall into despair. I will always feel deep pain – for those of us who were victims – but also for the perpetrators. Certainly, we victims were deeply harmed. However, I wonder how those who committed the hideous crimes could possibly live as though nothing had happened. There is no way I would have wanted to change positions with my torturers.

Therefore, I no longer feel hatred toward them, but rather I feel pity and a kind of compassion for them.

* NOTE: Parts of this chapter have been taken from *Towers of Hope* by Joy Carol with Anna's permission.

SUKHBIR and SARGUM SINGH

Practicing Love and Generosity

The Kindness and Bigheartedness of Sikhism

All human beings are the reflection of one and the same Lord.
Recognize the entire human race as one.
-- Sri Guru Gobind Singh Ji

In the late 15th century, Sikhism originated in the Punjab region of the Indian subcontinent. Sikhs share a common religious and ethnic background and an open and inclusive faith. Most of the 25-30 million Sikh members live in the Punjab, where the main seat of Sikh religious authority is located.

The core beliefs of Sikhism include faith and meditation in the name of the one Creator; divine equality and unity of all humankind; engaging in selfless service; striving for justice for the benefit and prosperity of all; and having an honest conduct and livelihood. Sikhs believe in one God and that all human beings are equal before God. They reject caste systems and the worship of idols. The meaning of the word "Sikh" is derived from the names "disciple," "learner," or "student."

Sikh members follow the tradition of selfless service ingrained in their community. Their founder Guru Nanak preached that selfless service (seva) and hard work are as important as prayer. At disasters, one may find Sikh volunteers helping victims, feeding the hungry, or rebuilding homes.

The spiritual site of Sikhism, the Golden Temple, is located in the city of Amritsar, India. It is open to people of all faiths and religions. Its four entrances symbolize the Sikh belief in equality, and that all people are welcome into their holy place. One building contains the largest free kitchen in the world. Open 24 hours a day, year round, this kitchen feeds for free 100,000 people without discrimination every day.

In the following delightful chapter is the lovely story of Sukhbir and Sargum Singh, whose caring and kindhearted lives reflect the teachings and practices of Sikhism.

Sukhbir and Sargum's Story

In our 28 years of living in Jacksonville, we know that we can be of different faiths and worldviews yet do significant work together.

We came to Jacksonville, Florida, in 1996 knowing little about the community to which we were moving. While we were interested in learning about our new community, we also felt compelled to teach the community about Sikhism. It was easy to see that Jacksonville had much to learn about our faith.

Whenever we've been given the opportunity, we have taught others about being a Sikh. We've spoken in schools and partnered with the Jacksonville Sheriff's Office educating as to our practices (including why we wear turbans). I (Sukhbir) even participated in the FBI Citizen's Academy. We hosted several "Wear a Turban" days on the campus of the University of North Florida (UNF). It is a fun way of teaching others the ways of our faith.

The foundational belief of our faith is that there is one God and everyone who worships worships the same God. This belief allows freedom to learn from others while also breeding an intellectual curiosity of other faiths and their practices.

Sikhism is a model for multi-faith cooperation. Our educational opportunities have also allowed us to speak in front of various faith communities. We've participated in synagogues, churches, and other institutions.

So, while learning about others in Jacksonville, we also began to offer times of prayer in our home. It was humbling and remarkable how people chose to join with us. There is power in being a member of a practicing community of faith. It is our responsibility to pray on our own, but sitting in a congregation is where we find divine vibrations to practice and serve. And service is where we choose to give the most profound witness of our faith.

We believe that when one sees a need, one should do everything in her or his power to meet it. Hunger is an issue that is always present in most communities. We found Jacksonville to be no different. We spend significant time trying to alleviate hunger in Jacksonville.

While meeting with our friends at OneJax, we happened to walk by the UNF food pantry called Lend-a-Wing. As it turns out, there is significant food insecurity among college students and Lend-a-Wing serves students at UNF. When we saw the opportunity, we acted. Our Gurudwara sisters and brothers acted with us. During Covid, we ran "Share a Meal." We regularly collected food and brought it to the UNF campus. Our food collection efforts expanded to the homeless center in Jacksonville, the Sulzbacher Center, and the St. Augustine School of the Deaf and Blind.

Not only does collecting food meet needs, it also speaks to our beliefs. It is imperative that those who have share with those who do not. It is in sharing that we practice equality and participate in the healing of our society. What a powerful symbol it is when sisters and brothers share a meal from a common kitchen!

It is this equality and generosity that is what we've learned from being Sikhs. There should be no discrimination among people in regards to wealth, gender, nor any other differences.

So, we continue our work – to bring everyone together. Not overlooking differences, but seeing the power of being together.

Ek Pita, Ekas Ke Hum Barik (p. 612, Sri Guru Granth Sahib [SGGS], sacred book of the Sikhs) – "One God is our father; we are His children."

We close this, as always, seeking, Tere Bhaane Sarbat Da Bhala – "Well being for all."

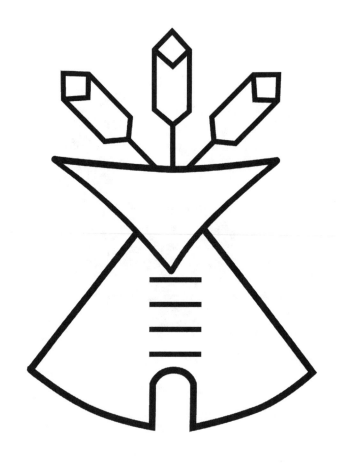

TULLEY SPOTTED EAGLE BOY
Feeling the Power of the Great Spirit
A Native American Shaman

*A very good vision is needed for life, and the man who has it
must follow it as the eagle seeks the deepest blue of the sky.*
- Chief Crazy Horse

How moving to see the Native American man, Tulley Spotted
Eagle Boy, walk proudly down the aisle of the Cathedral of St.
John the Divine in New York City during worship services. This
tall Mi'Kmaq medicine man had suffered greatly, somehow
survived, and had found significance and meaning in his life.

Tulley's story is filled with losses, pain, abuse, addiction. However, it also includes a powerful transformation of hope and
optimism. Tulley and his Native American brothers and sisters
were deeply wounded – particularly by white people.

But during his pain and suffering, Tulley was blessed to receive wisdom and guidance from caring people who helped
him learn to forgive the many who had hurt him – and also to
forgive himself. With support and love, he was able to reclaim
his authentic self and discover what he was meant to do with
his precious life.

Tulley Spotted Eagle Boy's story clearly shows that when
brokenness or anger go unhealed, they can become a toxic
poison to one's self, society, and the world. However, as Tulley
would say, clearing hatred from one's heart can make room
for the "Great Spirit." Then resolution, forgiveness, and understanding can develop.

Eventually, Tulley gained a vision of service and reconciliation for his community, the world, and for peoples of all faiths.

Tulley's Story

As a child, I grew up in a place where there were forests, animals, and fish. I felt a part of the earth and in touch with nature and animals. I was blessed to be one with them.

When I was four or five, an Indian agent came to our home on the reserve and took my three brothers, three sisters, and me away from our parents. We were put on a huge iron monster, which I was told was a train. When we left the station, I looked out the window and saw my mother crying.

We were taken to a residential school, where our hair was cut off, and we were scrubbed with wire brushes. I only knew my language of Mi'Kmaq. We were denied our language and culture. Sisters and brothers were separated from each other and weren't allowed to receive things from the outside world. We only saw our parents once a year. For years we went through misery and pain.

By the time I was nine, I drank anything to escape my sorrow. At fourteen, I left school and went back home to the reserve as an alcoholic. I drank every day. I couldn't deal with what had happened. My culture, identity, pride, and spirit had been taken from me. What I had left was guilt and shame.

Many native people couldn't live with that. Some children went home to find their parents were alcoholics. They thought they had done something wrong since their children had been taken away from them. They felt humiliation and disgrace.

On the reserve, I continued to drink and use drugs. When I was 22 years old, I went fishing with a friend in the Miramichi River. In my drunken state, I fell overboard and nearly drowned. I had a vision of my grandfather telling me that I had work to do for the people and for the earth, that I would be given sacred powers to help in my work.

After that, I began to wonder if there might be a Creator who was watching over me. Later, I learned the Great Spirit does watch over all of us – no matter who we are.

Until I was 24, I continued to drink anything with alcohol – rubbing alcohol, perfume, Lysol, shaving lotion. I wanted to forget the shame I had experienced. I was known as the "reserve drunk" and an embarrassment to my family, my people, to the whole Miramichi people – and to myself.

One day I was very hung over and sick with the DTs (delirium tremens). My sister asked me to take care of her daughter, Oasaweg, while she went to the store. I asked her to bring me a bottle of shaving lotion or anything to calm my nerves.

Because I couldn't stay still, my niece and I went for a walk. I fell to the ground and started shaking with cold sweats and nausea. I needed a drink. I started to cry. My niece asked, "What's wrong, Uncle?" I looked at her and said, "I am sick and tired of being sick and tired. All this alcohol, drinking, and other stuff are killing me." She said, "Uncle, why don't you pray?"

So, I asked the Great Spirit to give me help. A warm feeling came over me. When I looked up, I saw an eagle above us. Standing up, I felt like something had been lifted from my soul, and I didn't seem to crave alcohol.

When my sister returned, she hadn't found any shaving lotion. I told her I wouldn't need it. She was surprised, because I was a chronic alcoholic who would drink anything. From then on, I never touched a drink. Now it's many years later. What a blessing from the Great Spirit!

The next day I left the reservation and went to Prince Edward Island to visit my brother George Paul, who had been an alcoholic – as were all my brothers and sisters. But eventually every one of us stopped drinking and got on with our spiritual lives. I stayed a year with George Paul, who gave me support and nourishment. He helped guide me toward my native spirituality – respect for all living things, Mother Earth, and all peoples of the human race.

While there, I received my Mi'Kmaq spirit name, Spotted

Eagle Boy. It's a great responsibility to have such a power-ful name. The spotted eagle is a sacred bird sitting near the Creator. I knew I must walk the talk and keep myself clean and sober.

One day I hitchhiked to Montana. On the way, I met a Sioux medicine man, who took me to his home. He told me, "I'm adopting you as my grandson. I will teach you ways that will help many people as you go on your journey." For the next two and a half years, he taught me what would happen on a vision quest and how to prepare for it.

One day, my adopted grandfather took me up on a mountain. He left me there for four days. "Grandson, you are on a vision quest, so I want you to take out your sacred pipe and call the eagle."

With great feelings in my heart, I sat alone on the mountain. I forgot about myself as I prayed for other people – children who were suffering and starving, the elderly, animals, and Mother Earth. And I prayed for the people who had hurt me. One night the Spirit told me that I would be given wisdom and sacred gifts, and I would be told how to use them.

That year was a very difficult year for the Mi'Kmaqs. I knew my people were suffering with problems of alcoholism and drug use.

The following year, when I went to the mountain for my vi-sion quest, I knew I needed to do something for my people – to help them with their pain, guilt, and shame. I asked the Great Spirit what I could do to help make things better for the Mi'Kmaq people.

On the mountain, I saw a vision of a beautiful log building on a hill overlooking the Miramichi River. There were activities, dances, and ceremonies in the building, and many people us-ing it – from children to elders. The building was to be a place for people to receive comfort, healing, and spiritual food. It was to be the Mother Earth Lodge, and it would help people who suffered from drug and alcohol addiction. It would be a spiritual center open to all peoples of all races, cultures, and faiths – not just the native people living at Red Bank First Na-tion.

113

After seven years of travels. I was back at the Red Bank Reserve. I was 32. When I left at 25, I stole, I was a drunk, and I almost never had on clean clothes. That was how people knew me. But my whole life had turned around. I had a second chance, a new beginning.

I had regained my strength, my language, my culture. And I had recovered my spirit and my spirituality. There were many elders, medicine people, and others who helped me along the way.

As I shared my vision of the Mother Earth Lodge, many people, including the leaders and the elders, had also gone through hardships and suffering, so they were open and supportive of my vision. Some offered to help support the costs of the Lodge. Soon we started planning the building of the Lodge.

Looking back, I understand why I was bitter toward white people. It felt like they had tried to take our spirit and our land, and to kill our buffalo. However, if we walk around with hatred in our hearts, we pass that on to innocent children or people.

When I work with people who have had much taken from them, I tell them that in spite of what may have happened, the Great Spirit has good ideas for everyone in this world.

Because of the Great Spirit's teachings, we must forgive and work with those who have hurt us. Those teachings are in our hearts and our spirits. If we can forgive, there will be no hatred as we live, and we can work with a clear mind and spirit.

Yes, there is always hope and something good. If we look for it, we can find it. It is possible to get out of a negative place and step into another place of goodness, healing, and wellness – for ourselves and for all people.

* NOTE: Parts of this chapter have been taken from *Towers of Hope* by Joy Carol with Tulley Spotted Eagle Boy's permission.

MOVING FORWARD

Coming together is a beginning. Keeping together is progress.
Working together is success.
– Henry Ford

In this time of global and collective challenges, we desperately need cooperation and collaboration of all peoples – despite their differences. In order to begin to address and solve some of our difficulties and problems, it is essential that we develop honest relationships that cross cultural, religious, and national borders. We all live on the same planet and breathe the same air. And we are all part of one world and thus should embrace each other and revel in our diversity. Therefore, it is critical for us to find a way to consciously seek out and embrace our shared humanity and concerns.

It has been seen in every chapter of this book that it is possible to develop supportive and constructive relationships that include respect, forgiveness, and joy in each other's profound differences. From these examples, we can learn what it means to appreciate and delight in the gift of diversity. The bonds described in these chapters exemplify the importance of openness and curiosity, love and forgiveness.

These true-life accounts show that knowing people who are different from us does make our lives richer and more meaningful. The inspiring examples of friendship and respect between people of diverse backgrounds and cultures remind us that we are all part of an interdependent web of existence and also show us ways to bridge great divides. By being open to exploring the spiritual journey of other people's cultures, faiths, and traditions, we may find that our own world view is enriched. And we may be pleasantly surprised by what we share in common.

Interestingly, a positive and somewhat unexpected outcome of personally knowing people who follow diverse cultural or religious paths may be a personal spiritual growth in one own's faith.

Joy Carol is an author, workshop/retreat leader, preacher, spiritual companion, and national speaker. Her recent books include Nine Lives of Joy; Seasons of Joy; The Fabric of Friendship; Stevie, the Wonder Cat; Journeys of Courage; Finding Courage; and Towers of Hope (Sorin Books, Ave Maria Press, Veritas).

Joy writes a spiritual blog at www.joycarol.com. Over the last 30 years, Joy has been an educator (Outstanding Young Educator of the USA), psychological counselor, founder of a women's center in NY, and manager of development programs around the world. She has worked in the developing world for the UNDP, Save the Children, Ford Foundation, United Methodist Global Ministries, and Child Fund (formerly Christian Children's Fund). She developed the first on-the-ground development program in Vietnam following the war.

Joy loves people; enjoys speaking, preaching, leading retreats and workshops; likes to garden, read, travel; appreciates classical to jazz music; and sings whenever possible. She is thrilled to be publishing her ninth book. Several years ago, Joy was challenged by Paraneoplastic Syndrome and is fortunate to be alive and under the care of Mayo Clinic (See YouTube Joy Carol Mayo Health). This has not stopped Joy's activities nor her passion for life.

(Website: www.joycarol.com)

Kyle Reese is the Chief Executive Officer of OneJax and former pastor of Hendricks Avenue Baptist Church in Jacksonville, Florida.

In his role, Kyle focuses on the strategic direction of the agency as well as connecting with the greater Jacksonville community. Bringing diverse people together is what OneJax is about and what Kyle enjoys most.

Kyle is a graduate of Leadership Jacksonville (Class of 2008) and participated in Leadership Florida Class XXVIII. Kyle serves on the board of Baptist Health and is currently chair of Baptist's Social Responsibility Committee. He holds degrees from Wayland University, George W. Truett Theological Seminary at Baylor University, and Northern Seminary.

At the end of 2023, Kyle will step down from his position to follow his calling to return to the pulpit as Senior Minister at the First Baptist Church of Savannah.
kyle@onejax.org

Katie Sanborn-Price lives in NYC with her husband who is from Trinidad (speaking of cultural diversity). She is the CFO of Private Security Protection Services, Inc., a security guard company that they have run together since 2014.
www.psp-nyc.com

She keeps in touch with her creative and musical roots by singing in a choir, dancing at every opportunity, and always having a creative project to work on.

This is the fourth book on which she has collborated with Joy Carol. And that is quite literally, cause for Joy.

Peace

Made in the USA
Columbia, SC
28 January 2024

30508145R00079